Mother of Sorrows

Mother of Sorrows

Richard McCann

LARGE PRINT

This large print edition published in 2005 by
RB Large Print
A division of Recorded Books
A Haights Cross Communications Company
270 Skipjack Road
Prince Frederick, MD 20678

Published by arrangement with Alfred A. Knopf,
a division of Random House, Inc.

This book is a work of fiction. Names, characters, places, and incidents
either are products of the author's imagination or are used fictitiously. Any
resemblance to actual events or locales or persons, living or dead, is
entirely coincidental.

Owing to limitations of space, all acknowledgements for
permission to print previously published material may be found at the
end of the book.

Publisher's Cataloging In Publication Data
(Prepared by Donohue Group, Inc.)

McCann, Richard.
   Mother of sorrows / Richard McCann.

   p. (large print) ; cm.

   ISBN: 1-4193-5428-0

1. Fatherless families—Fiction. 2. Mothers and sons—Fiction. 3. Suburban
life—Fiction. 4. Gay youth—Fiction. 5. Large type books. 6. Washington
(D.C.)—Fiction. 7. Historical fiction. 8. Domestic fiction. I. Title.

PS3563.A2575 M67 2005
813/.54

Printed in the United States of America

**This Large Print Book carries the
Seal of Approval of N.A.V.H.**

FOR MIMI—
MY FIRST WORD,
THE FIRST LOVE OF MY LIFE

And when the mother entered, as if in a dream,
a glass quaked in the silent china closet.
She felt it, how the room was betraying her,
and kissed her child, saying, "Are you here?"
Then both looked toward the piano in fear,
for often at evening they would have a song
in which the child found himself strangely caught.

—*Rainer Maria Rilke,* "From Childhood"

CONTENTS

CRÊPE DE CHINE

Each night, after dinner, my father went downstairs to his workbench to build birdhouses, which he fashioned from scraps of wood left over from pine-paneling our basement. He was a connoisseur of birdhouses, my mother said. His favorite was a miniature replica of our ranch house, with a tiny Plexiglas picture window, a red Dutch door, and a shingled roof. It was a labor of love, he said the night he completed it.

My brother, Davis, went to his room, where he listened to Radio Moscow on his shortwave. As for me: I cleared the table.

"Sit with me, son," my mother said. "Let's pretend we're sitting this dance out."

She told me I was her best friend. She said I had the heart to understand her. She was forty-six. I was nine.

She sat at the table as if she were waiting to be photographed, holding her cigarette aloft. "Have I told you the story of my teapot?" she asked, lifting a Limoges pot from the table. She had been given the teapot by her mother, whom we called Dear—*Dear One, Dear Me, Dearest of Us All*. Dear had just recently entered a sanatorium for depression, after having given away some of her most cherished possessions. When she died at home a few months later—she'd returned to her deteriorated Brooklyn brownstone, where she slept on a roll-away bed in the basement—my mother found she'd left an unwitnessed will written entirely in rhymed couplets: "I spent as I went / Seeking love and content," it began.

"No," I told my mother as I examined the teapot's gold-rimmed lid, "you haven't told me about it."

In fact, by then my mother had already told me about almost everything. But I wanted to hear everything again. What else in Carroll Knolls—our sunstruck subdivision of identical brick houses—could possibly have competed with the stories my mother would summon from her china or her incomplete sterling tea service or the violet Louis Sherry candy box where she kept her dried corsages? I wanted to live within the lull of her voice, soft and regretful, as she resuscitated the long-ago nights of her girlhood, those nights she waited for her parents to come home in taxicabs from parties, those nights they still lived in the largest house on Carroll Street, those nights before her parents' divorce, before her father started his drinking.

She whispered magic words: *crêpe de chine, Sherry Netherlands, Havilland, Stork Club, argent repousée . . .*

2

Night after night she told me her stories.

Night after night I watched her smoke her endless Parliaments, stubbing out the lipstick-stained butts in a crystal ashtray. We sat at the half-cleared table like two deposed aristocrats for whom any word might serve as the switch of a *minuterie* that briefly lights a long corridor of memory—so long, in fact, the switch must be pressed repeatedly before they arrive at the door to their room.

She said her mother had once danced with the Prince of Wales.

She said her father had shaken hands with FDR and Al Capone.

She said she herself had once looked exactly like Merle Oberon.

To prove it, she showed me photos of herself taken during her first marriage, when she was barely twenty. From every photo she'd torn her ex-husband's image, so that in most of them she was standing next to a jagged edge, and in some of them a part of her body—where he'd had his hand on her arm, perhaps—was torn away also.

She said life was fifty-fifty with happiness and heartache.

She said that when she was a girl she'd kept a diary in which she'd recorded the plots of her favorite movies.

She said that if I was lucky I too would inherit the gift of gab.

When I was little, she read me *Goodnight, Moon.*

Goodnight, nobody. Goodnight, mush. And goodnight to the old lady whispering "hush."

But otherwise, she read me no bedtime books. She told me no fairy tales.

Instead she came to my room at night to tell me stories that began like these: *Once upon a time, I had a gold brush and comb set. Once upon a time, my parents looked like F. Scott and Zelda Fitzgerald. Once upon a time, I rode a pony in Central Park. Once upon a time, I had a silver fox coat.*

Things she told me, sitting on the edge of my bed at night:

"I was born with a caul. That means I have a sixth sense."

Or, touching her perfumed wrist to my cheek: "This is called 'Shalimar.'"

Or, faintly humming: "Do you know this tune? Do you know 'When I Grow Too Old to Dream, I'll Have You to Remember'?"

Or sometimes when she coughed—her "nervous cough," her "smoker's cough"—she said, "One day, after I'm gone, you'll hear a woman cough like this, and you'll think she is me."

MY MOTHER'S CLOTHES: THE SCHOOL OF BEAUTY AND SHAME

Like every corner house in Carroll Knolls, the corner house on our block was turned backward on its lot, a quirk introduced by the developer of the subdivision, who, having run short of money, sought variety without additional expense. The turned-around houses, as we kids called them, were not popular, perhaps because they seemed too public, their casement bedroom windows cranking open onto sunstruck asphalt streets. In actuality, it was the rest of the houses that were public, their picture windows offering dioramic glimpses of early-American sofas and Mediterranean-style pole lamps with mottled globes hanging like iridescent melons from wrought-iron chains. In order not to be seen walking across the living room to the kitchen in our pajamas, we had to close the Venetian blinds. The corner house on our block was secretive, as though it had turned its back on all of us, whether in superiority or shame, refusing to acknowledge even its own unkempt yard of yellowing zoysia grass. After its initial occupants

5

moved away, the corner house remained vacant for months.

The spring I was in sixth grade, it was sold. When I came down the block from school, I saw a moving van parked at its curb. "Careful with that!" a woman was shouting at a mover as he unloaded a tiered end table from the truck. He stared at her in silence. The veneer had already been splintered from the table's edge, as though someone had nervously picked at it while watching TV. Then another mover walked from the truck carrying a child's bicycle, a wire basket bolted over its thick rear tires, brightly colored plastic streamers dangling from its handlebars.

The woman looked at me. "What have you got there? In your hand."

I was holding a scallop shell spray-painted gold, with imitation pearls along its edges. Mrs. Eidus, the art teacher who visited our class each Friday, had shown me how to make it.

"A hat pin tray," I said. "It's for my mother."

"It's real pretty." She glanced up the street as though trying to guess which house I belonged to. "I'm Mrs. Tyree," she said, "and I've got a boy about your age. His daddy's bringing him tonight, in the new Plymouth. I bet you haven't sat in a new Plymouth."

"We have a Ford," I told her. I studied her housedress, tiny blue and purple flowers imprinted on thin cotton, a line of white buttons as large as Necco Wafers marching toward its basted hemline.

6

She was the kind of mother my mother laughed at for cutting recipes out of *Woman's Day*. Staring from our picture window, my mother would sometimes watch the neighborhood mothers drag their folding chairs into a circle on someone's lawn. "There they go," she'd say, "a regular meeting of the Daughters of the Eastern Star!" "They're hardly even *women*," she'd whisper to my father. "And their *clothes*." She'd criticize their appearance—their loud nylon scarves tied beneath their chins, their disintegrating figures stuffed into pedal pushers—until my father, worried that my brother, Davis, and I could hear, though laughing himself, would beg her, "Stop it, Maria, please stop; it isn't funny." But she wouldn't stop, not ever. "Not even thirty, and they look like they belong to the DAR! They wear their pearls inside their bosoms in case the rope should break!" She was the oldest mother on the block, but she was the most glamorous, sitting alone on the front lawn in her sleek kick-pleated skirts and cashmere sweaters, reading her thick paperback novels, whose bindings had split. Her hair was lightly hennaed, so that when I saw her pillow-cases piled atop the washer, they seemed dusted with powdery rouge. She had once lived in New York City.

After dinner, when it was dark, I joined the other children congregated beneath the street lamp across from the turned-around house. Bucky Trueblood, an eighth grader who'd once twisted the stems off my brother's eyeglasses, was crouched in the center, describing his mother's naked body to us elementary school children gathered around him, our faces slightly upturned, as though searching for a distant constellation or for the bats that Bucky said would fly into our hair. I sat at the edge, one half of my body within the circle of light, the other half lost to darkness. When Bucky described his mother's nipples, which he'd glimpsed when she bent to kiss him good night, everyone giggled; but when he described her genitals, which he'd seen by dropping his pencil on the floor and looking up her nightie while her feet were propped on a hassock as she watched TV, everyone huddled nervously together, as though listening to a ghost story that made them fear something dangerous in the nearby dark. "I don't believe you," someone said. "I'm telling you," Bucky said, *that's what it looks like*".

I slowly moved outside the circle. Across the street a cream-colored Plymouth was parked at the curb. In a lighted bedroom window, Mrs. Tyree was hanging café curtains. Behind the chain-link fence, the new child was standing in his yard. I could see his white T-shirt and the pale oval of his face, a face deprived of detail by darkness and distance. Behind him, at the open bedroom window, his mother slowly fiddled with a valance. Behind me the children sat spellbound beneath the light. Then Bucky jumped up and pointed in the new child's direction—"Hey, you.

You want to hear something really *good?*"—and even before the others had a chance to spot him, he vanished as suddenly and completely as an imaginary playmate.

The next morning, as we waited at our bus stop, he loitered by the mailbox on the opposite corner, not crossing the street until the yellow school bus pulled up and flung open its door. Then he dashed aboard and sat down beside me. "I'm Denny," he said. Denny: a heavy, unbeautiful child, who, had his parents stayed in their native Kentucky, would have been a farm boy, but who in Carroll Knolls seemed to belong to no particular world at all, walking past the identical ranch houses in his overalls and Keds, his whitish-blond hair close-cropped all around except for the distinguishing, stigmatizing feature of a wave that crested perfectly just above his forehead, a wave that neither rose nor fell, a wave he tended fussily, as though it were the only loveliness he allowed himself.

What in Carroll Knolls might have been described by someone not native to those parts—a visiting expert, say—as *beautiful*, capable of arousing terror and joy? The brick ramblers strung with multicolored Christmas lights? The occasional front-yard plaster Virgin entrapped within a chicken-wire grotto entwined with plastic roses? The spring Denny moved to Carroll Knolls, I begged my parents to take me to a nightclub, had begged so

9

hard for months, in fact, that by summer they had finally agreed to a Sunday matinee. Waiting in the backseat of our Country Squire, a red bow tie clipped to my collar, I watched our house float like a mirage behind the sprinkler's web of water. The front door opened, and a white dress fluttered within the mirage's ascending waves: slipping on her sunglasses, my mother emerged onto the concrete stoop, adjusted her shoulder strap, and teetered across the wet grass in new spectator shoes. Then my father stepped out and cut the sprinkler off. We drove—the warm breeze inside the car sweetened by my mother's Shalimar—past ranch houses tethered to yards by chain-link fences; past the Silver Spring Volunteer Fire Department and Carroll Knolls Elementary School; past the Polar Bear Soft-Serv stand, its white stucco siding shimmery with mirror shards; past a bulldozed red-clay field where a weathered billboard advertised, IF YOU LIVED HERE, YOU'D BE HOME BY NOW, until we arrived at the border—a line of cinder-block discount liquor stores, a traffic light—of Washington, D.C. The light turned red. We stopped. The breeze died and the Shalimar fell from the air. Exhaust fumes mixed with the smell of hot tar. A drunk man stumbled into the sidewalk, followed by an old woman shielding herself from the sun with an orange umbrella, and two teenage boys dribbling a basketball back and forth between them. My mother put down her sun visor. "Lock your door," she said.

Then the light changed, releasing us into another country. The station wagon sailed down boulevards of Chinese elms and flowering Bradford pears, through hot, dense streets where black families sat on wooden chairs at curbs, along streetcar tracks that caused the tires to shimmy and the car to swerve, onto Pennsylvania Avenue, past the White House, encircled by its fence of iron spears, and down Fifteenth Street, past the Treasury Building, until at last we reached the Neptune Room, a cocktail lounge in the basement of a shabbily elegant hotel.

Inside, the Neptune Room's walls were painted with garish mermaids reclining seductively on underwater rocks, and human frogmen who stared longingly through their diving helmets' glass masks at a loveliness they could not possess on dry earth. Onstage, leaning against the baby grand piano, a chanteuse (as my mother called her) was singing of her grief, her wrists weighted with rhinestone bracelets, a single blue spotlight making her seem like one who lived, as did the mermaids, under water.

I was transfixed. I clutched my Roy Rogers cocktail (the same as a Shirley Temple, but without the cheerful, girlish grenadine) tight in my fist. In the middle of "The Man I Love," I stood and struggled toward the stage.

I strayed into the spotlight's soft blue underwater world. Close up, from within the light, the singer was a boozy, plump peroxide blonde in a tight black cocktail dress; but these indiscretions made her yet more lovely, for they showed what she had lost, just as her songs seemed to carry her backward into endless regret. When I got close to her, she extended one hand—red nails, a huge glass ring—and seized one of mine.

"Why, what kind of little sailor have we got here?" she asked the audience.

I stared through the border of blue light and into the room, where I saw my parents gesturing, although whether they were telling me to step closer to her microphone or to step away, I could not tell. The whole club was staring.

"Maybe he knows a song!" a man shouted from the back.

"Sing with me," she whispered. "What can you sing?"

I wanted to lift her microphone from its stand and bow deeply from the waist, as I'd once seen Judy Garland do on a TV variety show. But I could not. As she began to sing, I stood voiceless, or, more accurately, I stood beside her, silently lip-synching to myself. I do not recall what she sang, although I do recall a quick, farcical ending in which she falsettoed, like Betty Boop, "Gimme a little kiss, will ya, huh?" and brushed my forehead with pursed red lips.

That summer, humidity enveloping the landfill subdivision, Denny, "the new kid," stood on the boundaries while we neighborhood boys played

War, a game in which someone stood on Stanley Allen's front porch and machine-gunned the rest of us, who one by one clutched our bellies, coughed as if choking on blood, and rolled in exquisite death throes down the grassy hill. When Stanley's father came up the walk from work, he ducked imaginary bullets. "Hi, Dad," Stanley would call, rising from the dead to greet him. Then we began the game again: Whoever had died best in the last round got to kill in the next. Later, after dusk, we'd smear the wings of balsa planes with glue, ignite them, and send them flaming down through the dark on kamikaze missions. Long after the streets were deserted, we children sprawled beneath the corner street lamp, praying our mothers would not call us— *"Time to come in!"*—back to our ovenlike houses; and then sometimes Bucky, hoping to scare the elementary school kids, would lead his solemn procession of junior high "hoods" down the block, their penises hanging from their unzipped trousers.

Denny and I began to play together, first in secret, then visiting each other's houses almost daily, and by the end of the summer I imagined him to be my best friend. Our friendship was sealed by our shared dread of junior high school. Davis, who had just finished seventh grade, brought back reports of corridors so long that one could get lost in them, of gangs who fought to control the lunchroom and the bathrooms. The only safe place seemed to be the health room, where a pretty nurse let you lie down on a cot behind a folding screen. Denny told me about a movie he'd seen in which the children, all girls, did not have to go to school at all but were taught at home by a beautiful governess, who, upon coming to their rooms each morning, threw open their shutters so that sunlight fell like bolts of satin across their beds, whispered their pet names while kissing them, and combed their long hair with a silver brush. "She never got mad," said Denny, beating his fingers up and down through the air as though striking a keyboard, "except once when some old man told the girls they could never play piano again."

With my father at work at the Pentagon and my mother off driving her two-tone Welcome Wagon Chevy to new subdivisions, Denny and I spent whole hours in the gloom of my living room, the picture window's Venetian blinds closed against an August sun so fierce it would bleach the design from the carpet. Dreaming of fabulous prizes—sets of matching Samsonite luggage, French provincial bedroom suites, Corvettes, jet flights to Hawaii—we watched Bud Collyer's *Beat the Clock* and Bob Barker's *Truth or Consequences* (a name that seemed strangely threatening). We watched *The Loretta Young Show*, worshipping yet critiquing her elaborate gowns. When *The Early Show* came on, we watched old Bette Davis, Gene Tierney, and Joan Crawford

14

movies—*Dark Victory, Leave Her to Heaven, A Woman's Face*. Hoping to become their pen pals, we wrote long letters to fading movie stars, who in turn sent us autographed photos we traded between ourselves. We searched the house for secrets, like contraceptives, Kotex, and my mother's hidden supply of Hershey bars. And finally, Denny and I, running to the front window every few minutes to make sure no one was coming unexpectedly up the sidewalk, inspected the secrets of my mother's dresser: her satin nightgowns and padded brassieres, folded atop pink drawer liners and scattered with loose sachet; her black mantilla, pressed inside a shroud of lilac tissue paper; her heart-shaped candy box, a flapper doll strapped to its lid with a ribbon, from which spilled galaxies of cocktail rings and cultured pearls. Small shrines to deeper intentions, private grottoes of yearning: her triangular cloisonné earrings, her brooch of enameled butterfly wings.

Because beauty's source was longing, it was infused with romantic sorrow; because beauty was defined as "feminine" and therefore as "other," it became hopelessly confused with my mother: Mother, who quickly sorted through new batches of photographs, throwing unflattering shots of herself directly into the fire before they could be seen. Mother, who dramatized herself, telling us and our playmates, "My name is Maria Dolores; in Spanish, that means 'Mother of Sorrows.'"

Mother, who had once wished to be a writer and who said, looking up briefly from whatever she was reading, "Books are my best friends." Mother, who read aloud from Whitman's *Leaves of Grass* and O'Neill's *Long Day's Journey into Night* with a voice so grave I could not tell the difference between them. Mother, who lifted cut-glass vases and antique clocks from her obsessively dusted curio shelves to ask, "If this could talk, what story would it tell?"

And more, always more, for she was the only woman in our house, a "people watcher," a "talker," a woman whose mysteries and moods seemed endless: Our Mother of the White Silk Gloves; Our Mother of the Veiled Hats; Our Mother of the Paper Lilacs; Our Mother of the Sighs and Heartaches; Our Mother of the Gorgeous Gypsy Earrings; Our Mother of the Late Movies and the Cigarettes; Our Mother whom I adored and whom, in adoring, I ran from, knowing it "wrong" for a son to wish to be like his mother; Our Mother who wished to influence us, passing the best of herself along, yet who held the fear common to that era, the fear that by loving a son too intensely she would render him unfit— "Momma's boy," "tied to apron strings"—and who therefore alternately drew us close and sent us away, believing a son needed "male influence" in large doses, that female influence was pernicious except as a final finishing, like manners; Our Mother of the Mixed Messages; Our Mother of

16

Sudden Attentiveness; Our Mother of Sudden Anger; Our Mother of Apology. The simplest objects of her life, objects scattered accidentally about the house, became my shrines to beauty, my grottoes of romantic sorrow: her Revlon lipstick tubes, "Cherries in the Snow"; her pastel silk scarves knotted to a wire hanger in her closet; her white handkerchiefs blotted with red mouths. Voiceless objects; silences. The world halved with a cleaver: "masculine," "feminine." In these ways was the plainest ordinary love made complicated and grotesque. And in these ways was beauty, already confused with the "feminine," also confused with shame, for all these longings were secret, and to control me all my brother had to do was to threaten to expose that Denny and I were dressing ourselves in my mother's clothes.

Denny chose my mother's drabbest outfits, as though he were ruled by the strictest of modesties, or by his family's austere Methodism: a pink wraparound skirt from which the color had been laundered, its hem almost to his ankles; a sleeveless white cotton blouse with a Peter Pan collar; a small straw summer clutch. But he seemed to challenge his own primness, as though he dared it with his "effects": an undershirt worn over his head to approximate cascading hair; gummed hole-punch reinforcements pasted to his finger-nails so that his hands, palms up, might look like

17

a woman's—flimsy crescent moons waxing above his fingertips.

He dressed slowly, hesitantly, but once dressed, he was a manic Proteus metamorphosing into contradictory, half-realized forms, throwing his "long hair" back and balling it violently into a French twist; tapping his paper nails on the glass-topped vanity as if he were an important woman kept waiting at a cosmetics counter; stabbing his nails into the air as though he were an angry teacher assigning an hour of detention; touching his temple as though he were a shy school-girl tucking back a wisp of stray hair; resting his finger-tips on the rim of his glass of Kool-Aid as though he were an actress seated over an ornamental cocktail—a Singapore sling, say, or a pink lady. Sometimes, in an orgy of jerky movement, his gestures overtaking him with greater and greater force, a dynamo of theatricality unleashed, he would hurl himself across the room like a mad girl having a fit, or like one possessed; or he would snatch the chenille spread from my parents' bed and drape it over his head to fashion for himself the long train of a bride. "Do you like it?" he'd ask anxiously, making me his mirror. "Does it look *real*?" He wanted, as did I, to become something he'd neither yet seen nor dreamed of, something he'd recognize the moment he saw it: himself. Yet he was constantly confounded, for no matter how much he adorned himself with scarves and jewelry, he could not understand that

18

this was himself, as was also and at the same time the boy in overalls and Keds. He was split in two pieces—as who was not?—the blond wave cresting rigidly above his close-cropped hair.

"He makes me nervous," I heard my father tell my mother one night as I lay in bed. They were speaking about me. That morning I'd stood awkwardly on the front lawn—"Maybe you should go help your father," my mother had said—while he propped an extension ladder against the house, climbed up through the power lines he separated with his bare hands, and staggered across the pitched roof he was reshingling. When his hammer slid down the incline, catching on the gutter, I screamed, "You're falling!" Startled, he almost fell.

"He needs to spend more time with you," I heard my mother say.

I couldn't sleep. Out in the distance a mother was calling her child home. A screen door slammed. I heard cicadas, their chorus as steady and loud as the hum of an electric substation. *He needs to spend more time with you.* Didn't she know? Saturday mornings, when he stood in his rubber hip boots fishing off the shore of Triadelphia Reservoir, I was afraid of the slimy bottom and could not wade after him; for whatever reasons of his own—something as simple as shyness, perhaps—he could not come to get me. I sat in the parking lot drinking Tru-Ade and reading *Betty andVeronica,* wondering if Denny had walked alone to Wheaton Plaza, where the weekend manager of Port-o'-Call allowed us to Windex the illuminated glass shelves that held Lladró figurines, the porcelain ballerina's hands so realistic one could see the tiny life and heart lines etched onto her palm. *He needs to spend more time with you.* Was she planning to discontinue the long summer afternoons that she and I spent together when there were no new families for her to greet in her Welcome Wagon car? "I don't feel like being alone today," she'd say, inviting me to sit on their chenille bedspread and watch her model new clothes in her mirror. Behind her an oscillating fan fluttered the nylons and scarves she'd heaped, discarded, on a chair. "Should I wear the red belt with this dress or the black one?" she'd ask, turning suddenly toward me and cinching her waist with her hands.

Afterward we'd sit together at the rattan table on the screened-in porch, holding cocktail napkins around sweaty glasses of iced Russian tea and listening to big band music on the Zenith.

"You look so pretty," I'd say. Sometimes she wore outfits I'd selected for her from her closet—pastel chiffon dresses, an apricot blouse with real mother-of-pearl buttons.

One afternoon she leaned over suddenly and shut off the radio. "You know you're going to leave me one day," she said. When I put my arms around her, smelling the dry carnation talc she wore in hot weather, she stood up and marched out of the room. When she returned, she was wearing Bermuda shorts and a plain cotton blouse. "Let's wait for your father on the stoop," she said.

That summer—the summer before he died—my father took me with him to Fort Benjamin Harrison, near Indianapolis, where, as a colonel in the U.S. Army Reserves, he did his annual tour of duty. On the prop jet he drank bourbon and read newspapers while I made a souvenir packet for Denny: an airsickness bag, into which I placed the Chiclets given me by the stewardess to help pop my ears during takeoff and the laminated white card that showed the location of emergency exits. Fort Benjamin Harrison looked like Carroll Knolls: hundreds of acres of concrete and sun-scorched shrubbery inside a cyclone fence. Daytimes, I waited for my father in the dining mess with the sons of other officers, drinking chocolate milk that came from a silver machine and desultorily setting fires in ashtrays. When he came to collect me, I walked behind him—gold braid hung from his epaulets—while enlisted men saluted us and opened doors. At night, sitting in our BOQ room, he asked me questions about myself: "Are you looking forward to seventh grade?" "What do you think you'll want to be when you grow up?" When these topics faltered—I stammered what I hoped were right answers—we watched TV, trying to preguess lines of dialogue on reruns of his favorite shows, *The Untouchables* and *Rawhide*. "That Della Street," he said as we watched *Perry Mason*, "is almost as pretty as your mother." On the last day, eager to make the trip memorable, he brought me a gift: a glassine envelope filled with punched IBM cards that told my life story as his secretary had typed it into the office computer. Card one: *You live at 10308 Lillians Mill Court, Silver Spring, Maryland*. Card two: *You are entering seventh grade*. Card three: *Last year your teacher was Mrs. Dillard*. Card four: *Your favorite color is blue*. Card five: *You love the Kingston Trio*. Card six: *You love basketball and football*. Card seven: *Your favorite sport is swimming*.

Whose son did these cards describe? The address was correct, as was the teacher's name and the favorite color; and he'd remembered that one morning during breakfast I'd put a nickel in the jukebox and played the Kingston Trio's song about "the man who never returned." But whose fiction was the rest? Had I, who played no sport other than kickball and Kitty-Kitty-Kick-the-Can, lied to him when he asked me about myself? Had he not heard from my mother the out-come of the previous summer's swim lessons? At the swim club a young man in black trunks had taught us, as we held hands, to dunk ourselves in water, surface, and then go down. When he had told her to let go of me, I had thrashed across the surface, violently afraid I'd sink. But perhaps I had not lied to him; perhaps he merely did not wish to see. It was my job, I felt, to reassure him that I was the son he imagined me to be, perhaps because the role of reassurer gave me power. In any case, I thanked him for the computer cards. I thanked him the way a father thanks a child for a well-intentioned gift he'll never use—a set of handkerchiefs, say, on which the embroidered swirls construct a monogram of no particular initial and which thus might be used by anyone.

As for me, when I dressed in my mother's clothes, I seldom moved at all: I held myself rigid before the mirror. The kind of beauty I'd seen practiced in movies and in fashion magazines was beauty attained by lacquered stasis, beauty attained by fixed poses—"ladylike stillness," the stillness of mannequins, the stillness of models "caught" in mid-gesture, the stillness of the passive moon around which active meteors orbited and burst. My costume was of the greatest solemnity: I dressed like the chanteuse in the Neptune Room, carefully shimmying my mother's black slip over my head so as not to stain it with Brylcream, draping her black mantilla over my bare shoulders, clipping her rhinestone dangles to my ears. Had I at that time already seen the movie in which French women who had fraternized with German soldiers were made to shave their heads and walk through the streets, jeered by their fellow villagers?

23

And if so, did I imagine myself to be one of the collaborators or one of the villagers taunting her from the curb? I ask because no matter how elaborate my costume, I made no effort to camouflage my crew cut or my male body.

How did I perceive myself in my mother's triple-mirrored vanity, its endless repetitions? I saw myself as doubled—both an image and he who studied it. I saw myself as beautiful, and guilty: the lipstick made my mouth seem the ripest rose, or a wound; the small rose on the black slip opened like my mother's heart disclosed, or like the Sacred Heart of Mary, aflame and pierced by arrows; the mantilla transformed me into a Mexican penitent, or a Latin movie star, like Dolores Del Rio. The mirror was a silvery stream: on the far side, in a clearing, stood the woman who was icily immune from the boy's terror and contempt; on the close side, in the bedroom, stood the boy who feared and yet longed after her inviolability. (Perhaps, it occurs to me now, this doubleness is the source of drag queens' vulnerable ferocity.) Sometimes, when I saw that person in the mirror, I felt as though I had at last been lifted from that dull, locked room, with its mahogany bedroom suite and chalky blue walls. But other times, particularly when I saw Denny and me together, so that his reality shattered my fantasies, we seemed merely ludicrous and sadly comic, as though we were dressed in the garments of another species, like dogs in human clothes. I became aware of my spatulate hands, my scarred knees, my large feet; I became aware of the drooping, unfilled bodice of my slip. Like Denny, I could neither dispense with images nor take their flexibility as pleasure, for the idea of self I had learned and was learning still was that one was constructed by one's image—"*When boys cross their legs, they cross one ankle atop the knee*"—so that one finally sought the protection of believing in one's own image and, in believing in it as reality, condemned oneself to its poverty.

(That locked room. My mother's vanity; my father's highboy. If Denny and I, still in our costumes, had left that bedroom, its floor strewn with my mother's shoes and handbags, and gone through the darkened living room, out onto the sunstruck porch, down the sidewalk, and up the street, how would we have carried ourselves? Would we have walked boldly, chattering extravagantly back and forth between ourselves, like drag queens refusing to acknowledge the stares of contempt that are meant to halt them? Would we have walked humbly, with the calculated, impervious piety of the condemned walking barefoot to the public scaffold? Would we have walked simply, as deeply accustomed to the normalcy of our strangeness as Siamese twins? Or would we have walked gravely, a solemn procession, like Bucky True-blood's gang, their manhood hanging from their unzipped trousers?

(We were eleven years old. Why now, decades

later, do I wonder for the first time how we would have carried ourselves through a publicness we would have neither sought nor dared? I am six feet, two inches tall. I weigh 195 pounds. Given my size, the question I am most often asked about my youth is "What football position did you play?" Overseas I am most commonly taken to be a German or a Swede. Right now, as I write this, I am wearing khaki trousers and an Oxford cloth shirt: an anonymous American costume, although partaking of certain signs of class and education, and, perhaps, partaking also of certain signs of sexual orientation, this costume having become one of the standard uniforms of the urban American gay man. Why do I tell you these things? Am I trying—not subtly—to inform us of my "maleness," to reassure us that I have "survived" without noticeable "complexes"? Or is this my urge, my constant urge, to complicate my portrait of myself to both of us, so that I might layer my selves like so many multicolored crinoline slips, each rustling as I walk? When the wind blows, lifting my skirt, I do not know which slip will be revealed.)

Sometimes, while Denny and I were dressing up, Davis would come home unexpectedly from the bowling alley, where he'd been hanging out since entering junior high. At the bowling alley he was courting the protection of Bucky's gang.

"Let me in," he'd demand, banging fiercely on

the bedroom door, behind which Denny and I were scurrying to wipe the makeup off our faces with Kleenex.

"We're not doing anything," I'd protest, buying time.

"Let me in this minute or I'll tell!"

Once in the room, Davis would police the wreckage we'd made, the emptied hatboxes, the scattered jewelry, the piled skirts and blouses. "You'd better clean this up right now," he'd warn. "You two make me *sick*."

Yet his scorn seemed modified by awe. When he helped us rehang the clothes in the closet and replace the jewelry in the candy box, a sullen accomplice destroying someone else's evidence, he sometimes handled the garments as though they were infused with something of himself, although at the precise moment when he seemed to find them loveliest, he would cast them down.

After our dress-up sessions Denny would leave the house without good-byes. I was glad to see him go. We would not see each other for days, unless we met by accident; we never referred to what we'd done the last time we'd been together. We met like those who have murdered are said to meet, each tentatively and warily examining the other for signs of betrayal. But whom had we murdered? The boys who walked into that room? Or the women who briefly came to life within it? Perhaps this metaphor has outlived its meaning. Perhaps our shame derived not from our having killed but from our having created.

In early September, as Denny and I entered seventh grade, my father became ill. Over Labor Day weekend he was too tired to go fishing. On Monday his skin had vaguely yellowed; by Thursday he was severely jaundiced. On Friday he entered the hospital, his liver rapidly failing; Sunday he was dead. He died from acute hepatitis, possibly acquired while cleaning up after our sick dog, the doctor said. He was buried at Arlington National Cemetery, down the hill from the Tomb of the Unknown Soldier. After the twenty-one-gun salute, our mother pinned his colonel's insignia to our jacket lapels. I carried the flag from the coffin to the car. For two weeks I stayed home with my mother, helping her write thank-you notes on small white cards with black borders; one afternoon, as I was affixing postage to the square, plain envelopes, she looked at me across the dining room table. "You and Davis are all I have left," she said. She went into the kitchen and came back. "Tomorrow," she said, gathering up the note cards, "you'll have to go to school."

Mornings I wandered the long corridors alone, separated from Denny by the fate of our last names, which had cast us into different homerooms and daily schedules. Lunchtimes we sat together in silence in the rear of the cafeteria. Afternoons, just before gym class, I went to the health room, where,

28

lying on a cot, I'd imagine the phys. ed. coach calling my name from the class roll, and imagine my name, unclaimed, unanswered to, floating weightlessly away, like a balloon that one jumps to grab hold of but that is already out of reach. Then I'd hear the nurse dial the telephone. "He's sick again," she'd say. "Can you come pick him up?" At home I helped my mother empty my father's highboy. "No, we want to save that," she said when I folded his uniform into a huge brown bag that read GOOD-WILL INDUSTRIES; I wrapped it in a plastic dry cleaner's bag and hung it in the hall closet.

As my mother retreated into her grief, she left behind only her mute objects as evidence of her life among us: objects that seemed as lonely and vulnerable as she was, objects that I longed to console, objects with which I consoled myself—a tangled gold chain, thrown in frustration on the mantel; a wineglass, its rim stained with lipstick, left unwashed in the sink. Sometimes at night Davis and I heard her prop her pillow against her bedroom wall, lean back heavily, and tune her radio to a call-in show. *"Nightcaps, what are you thinking at this late hour?"* Sunday evenings, in order to help her prepare for the next day's job hunt, I stood over her beneath the bare basement bulb, the same bulb that first illuminated my father's jaundice. I set her hair, slicking each wet strand with gel and rolling it, inventing gossip that seemed to draw us together, a beautician and his customer.

"You have such pretty hair," I'd say.

"At my age, don't you think I should cut it?" She was almost fifty.

"No, never."

That fall Denny and I were caught. One evening my mother noticed something out of place in her closet. (Perhaps now that she no longer shared it, she knew where every belt and scarf should have been.)

I was in my bedroom doing my French homework, dreaming of one day visiting Au Printemps, the store my teacher spoke of so excitedly as she played us the Edith Piaf records she had brought back from Paris. In the mirror above my desk I saw my mother appear at my door.

"Get into the living room," she said. Her anger made her small, reflected body seem taut and dangerous.

In the living room Davis was watching TV with Uncle Joe, our father's brother, who sometimes came to take us fishing. Uncle Joe was lying in our father's La-Z-Boy recliner.

"There aren't going to be any secrets in this house," she said. "You've been in my closet. What were you doing there?"

"No, we weren't," I said. "We were watching TV all afternoon."

"*We?* Was Denny here with you? Don't you think I've heard about that? Were you and Denny going through my clothes? Were you wearing them?"

"No, Mom," I said.

"Don't lie!" She turned to Uncle Joe, who was staring at us. "Make him stop! He's lying to me!"

She slapped me. Although I was already taller than she, she slapped me over and over, slapped me across the room until I was backed against the TV. Davis was motionless, afraid. But Uncle Joe jumped up and stood between my mother and me, holding her until her rage turned to sobs. "I can't be both a mother and a father," she said to him. "I can't, I can't do it." I could not look at Uncle Joe, who, although he was protecting me, did not know I was lying.

She looked at me. "We'll discuss this later," she said. "Get out of my sight."

We never discussed it. Denny was outlawed. I believe, in fact, it was I who suggested he never be allowed in our house again. I told my mother I hated him. I do not think I was lying when I said this. I truly hated him—hated him, I mean, for being me.

For two or three weeks Denny tried to speak with me at the bus stop, but whenever he approached, I busied myself with kids I barely knew. After a while Denny found a new best friend, Lee, a child despised by everyone, for Lee was "effeminate." His clothes were too fastidious; he often wore his cardigan over his shoulders, like an old woman feeling a chill. Sometimes, watching the street from our picture window, I'd see Lee walking toward Denny's house. "What a queer,"

I'd say to whoever might be listening. "He walks like a *girl*." Or sometimes, at the junior high school, I'd see him and Denny walking down the corridor, their shoulders pressed together as if they were telling each other secrets, or as if they were joined in mutual defense. Sometimes when I saw them, I turned quickly away, as though I'd forgotten something important in my locker. But when I felt brave enough to risk rejection, for I belonged to no group, I joined Bucky Trueblood's gang, sitting on the radiator in the main hall, and waited for Lee and Denny to pass us. As Lee and Denny got close, they stiffened and looked straight ahead.

"Faggots," I muttered.

I looked at Bucky, sitting in the middle of the radiator. As Lee and Denny passed, he leaned forward from the wall, accidentally disarranging the practiced severity of his clothes, his jeans puckering beneath his tooled belt, his T-shirt drooping with the weight of a packet of Pall Malls. He whistled. Lee and Denny flinched. He whistled again. Then he leaned back, the hard lines of his body reasserting themselves, his left foot striking a steady beat on the tile floor with the silver V tap of his black loafer.

DREAM HOUSE

The night Davis and I told our father we wanted a bomb shelter, I sat in silence at the dinner table, listening for sounds from my mother's bedroom. I watched my father butter his bread. I watched Davis sort through his 3-D cards, whose deep focal views—a fisherman with the Hoover Dam behind him, a comet flaming through the gaseous clouds of the Milky Way— were supposed to strengthen his lazy eye. He wore a brown patch taped to his glasses.

Then Davis stacked his cards into a pile and opened his *Superboy* comic. On its back cover, an advertisement pictured a boy laughing at a postman who was coming up the sidewalk, toting a heavy parcel that shouted, "Help! Help! I'm trapped inside!" YOU CAN LEARN TO THROW YOUR VOICE! the ad promised.

If Mom saw Davis reading in the dark, I thought, she would turn on a lamp. But since her mother's death the previous month, she had retreated to her bedroom.

"Turn on a lamp," I told Davis.

After dinner, our father watched a rerun of

33

Gunsmoke. Davis sat beside him, holding the booklet, *Your Survival in Nuclear Attack*, that the Civil Defense warden had distributed that afternoon at school. The first through sixth grades—Davis was in sixth; I was a year younger—had assembled in the school cafeteria. Then the warden turned off the lights and showed us a picture of a cloud surging violently upward, as though, though enormous pressure, it had suddenly released itself from the hard darkness of the earth's core. Yet as the cloud rose, it grew calmer, spreading out lazily in all directions, like summer cumulus carrying a dream-cargo of familiar faces. When the lights came on, some students told the warden what they'd seen within the mushroom cap: someone had seen Abe Lincoln's face as it appeared on a penny; someone had seen his mother's. It was a mistake, the warden said, to look at it like this. The cloud's tendency to drift was actually its greatest danger. He showed us pictures of cows lying dead in fields outside Hiroshima and Nagasaki.

"Boom!" Davis shouted as we walked home. As we turned onto our block, he began pretending the bomb had already fallen, and that he was weakening with each step taken, as if our house were somehow radioactive, although he'd said we were rushing toward its safety. By the time he reached our sidewalk, he was staggering on his knees, his arms outspread. When he got to the front stoop, he lurched and fell forward. "Water!" he cried. "Water! I must have water or I'll die!"

34

"Quiet," I said. "I think Mom's sleeping." Her Venetian blinds were drawn. The sprinkler, left on since morning, was coursing slowly back and forth, flooding the front lawn.

When our father got home from work, he made us one of his "bachelors' meals"—scrambled eggs with chopped-up hot dogs in them. Then he suggested we watch TV.

"Dad," Davis said, interrupting *Gunsmoke*. "We have to build a bomb shelter." He showed him a picture of a suburban family secure within their cement-block basement shelter. The parents looked as if they'd just come home from a cocktail party. The father, standing over his two sons asleep in bunk beds, was testing their radiation levels with a dosimeter. The mother, sitting on a daybed, was examining a selection of magazines fanned out across a Danish modern coffee table. The shelter was small and compact, like the Shasta travel trailer we'd rented the previous summer. My mother had hated the trailer, with its cramped interior, and its flimsy dinette that folded into a narrow double bed. But I had liked the way I would wake at night to the sound of everyone breathing.

"I'm watching my show," our father said. "Not now."

On *Gunsmoke*, Miss Kitty was being held captive in a livery stable by a madman who waved a gun in her face. "No," Miss Kitty swore, "you'll never make me tell!" She wore one of her beautiful dance hall dresses, lacy ruffles cascading from its bodice. She didn't know that Matt Dillon, who was supposed to save her, was lying wounded in the desert.

I heard my mother get up and click on the radio in her bedroom. It spilled out news. She turned the dial to *Make-Believe Ballroom*, broadcast nightly from a hotel in downtown Baltimore. The band was playing "Stardust"—"*Sometimes I wonder why I spend / the lonely night / dreaming of a song . . .*"

"The warden gave us a letter you have to sign," I told my father.

But he was watching TV, lost in his show. He is not prepared, I thought. He will be one of those people the warden warned us about, one of those people who imagine they'll have time to pack the car and drive away. "Nowhere's safer than our Country Squire," he'd once reassured Davis and me as we drove at night through lightning. But as he spoke, the headlights of an approaching car tore through our car's interior, illuminating the sudden boundaries of his body.

"The school has to know whether to keep us there or send us home when the bomb falls," I told him.

"You have to check a box on a note they gave us," Davis said. He began reading aloud from the Civil Defense booklet: "A dual-usage approach to shelter protection is highly desirable. The protected space can be used for other normal day-to-day activities, such as guest room, recreation room . . ."

"Look, Davis, there's Chester," our father said. Davis loved Chester, Matt Dillon's crippled deputy. Chester was the reason Davis watched *Gunsmoke*. The day our father built our log-cabin playhouse, Davis had limped around the back-yard, shouting, "Look, Dad! Look! I'm Chester!"

But now Davis was becoming panicked. He started crying.

My mother clicked off her radio. I heard her go into the bathroom and begin drawing her bath.

"All right, Davis, don't cry," our father said. "Let me see the letter."

"You have to tell Mom to buy food for the shelter," Davis told him. "You have to tell Mom to buy food in cans."

Our father unfolded the letter: "Dear Parents or Legal Guardians," he read aloud. Then he asked for a pen.

"Now let me watch my show," he said. When he handed the letter back to Davis, I saw he had checked the box that said "Go-Home Plan."

That night I lay awake for a long time, listening to people laugh on TV.

For a long time, I studied a white shirt that hung, faintly moving, on a wire hanger in my closet. The more I studied the white shirt, the more it seemed to sway, as though it were a speechless figure that wanted to whisper me its secret.

Shh, I wanted to whisper back. *Be quiet, be still.*

My mother's grief was traveling through the wall. As it entered, it penetrated every object in my room—the yellow curtains, the wooden wind chimes, the ticking clock. It gathered in the folds of my rumpled sheet, and everywhere my sheet touched me—along my legs, my upper arms—I could feel her grief's soft weight descending. The sheet grew heavy. It overwhelmed me. I pulled it tight and wrapped myself within it.

Then I heard "The Star-Spangled Banner" playing on TV.

"Come on, old boy," I heard my father say. "Let's make sure the doors are locked." He was talking to our cocker spaniel, Mickey.

The house grew quiet. I lay suspended within the loose web of my own breathing. For a moment I whispered my mother's name—*Maria, Maria*—but nothing happened. Then I started to wonder if she'd sleep late the next day, or if she'd get up early, as she had that morning, to say good-bye to Davis and me before we left for school. Weary and sleepless, she'd emerged from her bedroom, wearing her housecoat and slippers. She'd sat at the kitchen table.

I made her instant coffee. Meanwhile, she withdrew her mother's sterling compact from her housecoat pocket and studied herself in its foggy mirror, touching a fingertip to the flecks of dried mascara that still clung to her lashes.

"Whenever I looked at myself in the mirror," she said, "Dear used to tell me that beauty was only skin deep. I thought she was trying to tell me I was ugly." Dear was her mother—*Dear One, Dear Me, Dearest of Us All*. She had died after coming home from the sanatorium she had entered for depression.

From the kitchen window, I could see my mother's unwashed Welcome Wagon Chevy. The previous Memorial Day, my father had chauffeured us—the car was a two-tone convertible, turquoise and black, with WELCOME WAGON painted on each door—in a parade sponsored by the Wheaton Merchants Association. My mother had sat in back, on the folded convertible top, with Davis and me on either side of her, tossing plastic change purses—SAVE FOR YOUR DREAM HOUSE! SUBURBAN TRUST BANK—to families sitting along the curbs. Beneath her Welcome Wagon sash she'd worn a brilliant blue dress appliquéd with silver leaves.

At the breakfast table, she lit a Parliament.

"Don't smoke," Davis said. "It's not healthy."

"Don't tell her what to do," I said.

"Look," she said. She was turning Dear's compact in her hand. As she turned it, a shard of white light danced across the kitchen wall—then it lighted briefly on the chrome face of the clock before scurrying to the ceiling.

Davis whispered, "Don't you care if Mom smokes?"

"I put a holy card from Dear's funeral in a time capsule," I told my mother. It was true. Davis and

I had sometimes put wallet-sized photos of ourselves in old mayonnaise jars. Then we wrapped the jars in aluminum foil and buried them in the backyard so people of the future would find them and see what we had looked like.

"She's only hurting herself," Davis said loudly.

My mother looked at me. "Your first day of school," she said, "I watched you from my bedroom window as you walked up the hill in your red reversible jacket. When you got to the top, you stopped and took off your jacket. He's changed his mind, I thought. But you turned the jacket inside out and put it on again so that you were wearing the side that was blue. I watched you until your blue jacket disappeared into the woods."

"Did you watch me, too?" Davis said.

"Yes, I watched you, too."

After school, Davis and I went down to the laundry room to begin the bomb shelter. We cleared our father's workbench of the birdhouses he was building. In their place, we spread our roughly drawn floor plan for a six-by-nine-foot bunker, with a right-angled baffle wall to protect us from deadly radiation's unbending light.

"Put down the masking tape," Davis said.

I laid masking tape along the floor to mark where the cinder-block walls would go. Within the taped borders, Davis chalked outlines of the furniture we'd planned—two sets of bunk beds, a table and four chairs, and a garbage can that would serve as our toilet. We tried to decide if we should hang draperies along one wall, to give us the illusion of having a picture window, an idea I'd once seen in *House Beautiful*.

"We have to have food," I said. At first, I tried to think of foods my mother might like, but then I felt I ought to hurry—we were working quickly, as if the bomb were already coming—so I copied a list of provisions from *Your Survival in Nuclear Attack*: sweetened condensed milk, nonfat dry milk, Spanish rice (canned), Chicken-'n'-Dumplings (canned), fruit cocktail (cans or glass jars), creamed corn, wax beans, strawberry jam, canned heat (STERNO) . . . According to the booklet, our family's survival would depend on strengthening our ability to anticipate all manner of emergencies: We'd need spare blankets, of course, and a transistor radio with a backup set of batteries.

But first we would have to establish a regular schedule for family conferences, in which we could sit down to discuss our needs quite openly, so we could plan for disaster accordingly. For instance, we'd need to determine the sorts of things that might maintain our morale, such as the playing of Old Maid and Parcheesi. In later sessions, we'd need to assess the psychological pressures we'd face due to sickness, confinement, and rationing, and to reach at least some tentative accord as to whether we should shoot our family dog for reasons of sanitation. Finally, we would even need to decide what we would do if one of us should

41

die, and to determine if we felt it was necessary to arm ourselves against our neighbors, including the women and children.

When Davis finished with the chalk, he told me to bring the booklet and get into the shelter. I followed the masking-tape line that outlined the baffle wall. I turned the corner and sat on the concrete floor.

Davis read from the booklet: "Some people believe that if they are exposed to radiation, they will immediately become 'walking stoves,' emitting radiation and endangering all those with whom they come into contact. True or false?"

I didn't know the answer. Above us, in her bedroom, I could hear our mother rearranging furniture, making room for a Victorian shaving stand she'd inherited from Dear.

"Close your eyes," Davis said.

I closed my eyes and thought about Dear. The last time we'd seen her, she had moved into the basement of her deteriorating Brooklyn brownstone—none of the upstairs bathrooms still worked. She'd sat on a roll-away bed, clutching the black handbag in which she kept what she called her "serious jewelry."

"I thought you'd decided not to visit me," she'd said to our mother. Across the bed she had spread old manila envelopes, which she'd secured with ancient rubber bands. She said she had been working on a letter to some lawyer who wanted to harm her.

Her dinner service came to us—Limoges, for thirty-six.

"Dear always tried to buy happiness," my mother once told me, fixing her hair with Dear's monogrammed gold brush. *Oh, well, happiness*—now our house was filling with antiques and stray objects that seemed barely freed from the close air of Dear's diminished life: twin cut-glass vases, stuffed with dusty artificial roses; a brass statuette of a fallen gladiator, which Dear had kept by her bed. *Well, happiness*—now my mother spent hours in her room, sorting through Dear's effects: a paper bag filled with soiled lace collars; a print of a sullen Baby Jesus, "The Light of the World"; a violet Louis Sherry candy box overflowing with costume jewelry, cocktail rings, and fancy brooches fashioned from glass as blue and lurid as a doll's opened eyes.

But there would be no room for these things in the shelter. We will have to be like pioneers, I thought, casting the heavy load from our covered wagon so we can ford the rising river. I shifted and opened my eyes. There was Davis, sitting beside me. But there was no shelter. There was only the laundry room—the workbench, the Maytag, the ragbag hanging from a nail in the wall.

"What is it?" Davis asked.

"Nothing."

"Then keep your eyes closed. Imagine what it will be like."

At first, I could not envision it. The basement smelled musty. It smelled of the firewood and old newspapers our father had stacked beneath the stairs.

Then it came: I saw the fireball, the blast surge, and the white cloud rising. I leaned back against the wall. I saw us in the shelter, waiting the long weeks for fallout to settle. I saw us climbing the basement stairs and opening the door onto the bright light of a world made immaculate by a force greater than ten suns. I knew then that the world that would await us was not a world of charred remains and ghastly rubble, like the photos the Civil Defense warden had shown us of orphans digging through the ashes of Hiroshima. Our world would not be so much destroyed as tranquilized. Our world would be new again.

Our world would be so new, in fact, that we would be able to choose a car—any car, a Thunderbird convertible, say—and drive all the way across the country to San Francisco. Our father would sing as he drove. He would put the top down. Our mother would untie her nylon scarf and let her hair fly freely in the breeze. She'd say, "Let's sit in back, boys, and have our own private parade," and the three of us would sit there, waving to no one—waving to the sea and sky, waving to the dream-clouds—as we crossed the Golden Gate Bridge. When we arrived, we'd find the city intact, a Lost Colony whose settlers had disappeared with no sign of struggle or distress, and we, the earth's last inhabitants, the born again, would wander down its broad avenues—avenues as clean and quiet and empty as the Grand Canyon. There would be no sound of weeping.

What did I imagine—that my mother would be restored to us, at last released from the spell of a past I believed she still loved more than anything? Or did I simply think she'd die of grief? Sometimes, on my way home from school, I stopped at Wheaton Florists, where, for twenty-five cents, I could buy three long, imperfect stems of gladiolus.

I carried them home, their red blooms flaring inside green tissue.

"Mom," I called out, pressing our front door buzzer like a delivery boy. But she didn't answer.

I went down to the shelter, where Davis helped me fill emptied Clorox bottles with fresh water—a drop of bleach left in an unrinsed Clorox bottle, I had read, would extend the water's shelf life to infinity, almost.

But each time we asked our father when we could actually begin the shelter's construction, he said only, "Don't talk about the shelter to your mother." He told us she was too tired; he told us she wasn't herself yet. He said she might take the train to New York City, as she'd done each month when Dear was sick, so she could see Charmaine, her baby sister. "We'll still have fun," he promised as he cooked dinner. "We'll go to the Enchanted Forest."

But at night I sometimes heard them arguing. "Dear was my *family*," my mother insisted.

"Then I guess I'm the one who should leave," he answered.

Afterward, I'd hear her in the kitchen, listening to the radio. *Mom*, I thought, as though I might possess a clairvoyant's power to reach her even through silence—to say what? *Mom*, I thought, over and over—*Mom, Mom.*

"I think Mom's almost better," I told Davis one afternoon. I was sitting within the shelter's masking-tape lines, memorizing the air-raid warning system from *Your Survival in Nuclear Attack:* The "red signal," a rising and falling siren lasting three minutes, meant take immediate cover; the "white signal," three one-minute siren blasts with intervals between them, meant all clear. Davis was water-proofing kitchen matches by dipping them in melted wax, a trick he'd read about in *Boys' Life.*

"No, she's the same," Davis said. Increasingly, he seemed annoyed with her. Sometimes when she came to his room to say good night he didn't answer his door. She'd tap again lightly—*Davis, Davis.*

He gathered the matches into a pile. "Anyway, it doesn't really matter," he said. He lit a match and blew it out. Then he lit another.

"Davis," I said.

"It's true," he said suddenly, dropping a match

46

to the concrete floor, where it kept burning. Then he said, "If they split up, I'd rather live with Dad."

I didn't know what to say. I thought of our mother sitting upstairs, unprotected. Each afternoon, when I came home from school, I'd find her sitting in her wing chair, reading one of her paperback novels—*Marjorie Morningstar*, or *The Robe*. Sometimes she seemed the lonely empress of a lost kingdom; other times, she simply seemed tired and old, like Dear. One day the sirens will go off, I thought. She will look up briefly, confused by a disturbance she doesn't understand. Then she will turn the page of her novel. She'll go on reading.

I looked at Davis. "You shouldn't even think like that," I told him.

We collected the waterproofed matches and stored them in a metal Band-Aid box. Then we went outside. It was only two o'clock. But the sky was already darkening, filling quickly with dense smoke.

"We'd better hurry," Davis said. In the woods that bordered our development, the Wheaton Volunteer Fire Department was burning the Haunted House for practice.

By the time we arrived, the Haunted House, as we kids called it—it was actually a wooden farmhouse, abandoned so long ago that no one knew who had lived there—was already burning. When I saw it, I thought of the phrase *out of control*. But

47

then I saw the firemen were busily hosing the underbrush and scrub pines so the fire wouldn't spread to the woods.

"That house is a mess," I heard a woman say.

"It's about time someone burned it," the woman behind her agreed. She said she hated even to imagine the poor woman who'd once lived there, whoever she was, because a house like that was a monster, a real ten-ton dust trap. She said her own house—a split-foyer, in a nearby sub-division—had an all-electric kitchen and two sliding glass doors.

"That's certainly much nicer," another woman added. They were talkative and festive, as if they'd come to the grand opening of a shopping center. Some mothers were pushing strollers.

While they talked, the Haunted House burned. I thought of the summer afternoons when Davis and I had played there, sitting in its cool dirt-floored cellar, where we'd found what looked like butterfly nets, or combing its vine-choked yard for blue medicine bottles and dinosaur bones. Once we'd even found a pair of broken spectacles beneath the front steps. "Put on those glasses," my mother told us when we brought them home, "and you'll see through a dead man's eyes."

Now the Haunted House would be replaced by a cluster of split-levels.

"Look!" a boy shouted. An upstairs window suddenly exploded. Then all the windows went, one by one, like gunshot blasts. "Stand back! Clear away!" the firemen shouted. They moved forward to hose the roof, but the roof had collapsed onto the walls.

I looked up. Sparks were flying backward, over our heads, carried into the woods by a gentle breeze. Whichever way the wind blows, I thought, the fallout will find us. It will rise and gather in rain clouds. It will fall in clean rain. No one will see it or feel it. No one will know what has happened until it's too late.

I looked at the house—it was quickly burning. Each time a smoking timber fell, it hissed in a pool of water the firemen had hosed, and the crowd hissed back in imitation. Meanwhile, the ash kept blowing backward, over our heads, back through the woods, back through the streets, back over the power lines and onto the roofs of our houses and the elementary school. I knew where it was heading. It was falling through the high limbs of our willow tree. It was catching on our window screens. It was drifting through our screened-in porch like black snow.

When we got home, our mother was not in her bedroom.

She was in the kitchen, making spaghetti. She had set the table with a red-checked cloth and an empty Chianti bottle into which she'd placed a red candle. She was holding her highball glass— part of a set that Dear had given her, a dozen matched pieces, each imprinted with the seal of

49

Monaco to celebrate the marriage of Princess Grace.

She turned to greet us. "Let's sit in the living room," she said.

"Not now," Davis told her. He said he needed to listen to his shortwave.

It was almost five o'clock. I knelt with my mother on the living room sofa, facing backward so we could look out the picture window. Across the street, Linda Garber was sitting on her front stoop, brushing her baby doll's hair.

"They burned the Haunted House," I told my mother. I wanted to ask if she remembered the time we'd found the broken spectacles and how she had told us that we could see through a dead man's eyes.

She lit a cigarette. She said, "When I was a child, I'd sit in the front window and wait for my father to come home. My mother always told me you had to wish the next car would be his. You really had to wish it. Then, if it wasn't the next car, it would be the one after that."

She said that had happened a long time ago, in the time before her parents separated. After their separation, she said, her parents saw each other only one more time, "like ships that pass in the night."

But at dinner, she was silent. Our father pushed his food back and forth on his plate. "It's a wonderful dinner," he said. "It's very good."

"Dinner's really good," I repeated. But I was watching Davis, who was watching our mother.

Then Davis stopped eating. He set down his knife and fork. "Dad," he said, "supposing a bomb falls and you can't get home from work in time?"

"Davis," our father said.

"Dear was terrified of German dirigibles," our mother said. "During the war, she installed blackout curtains on every window in our house. My uncle Carl was the block warden—'There go the sirens, Maria, shut the curtains before Uncle Carl walks by and catches us!' It was romantic. We sat in the dark and listened to Frank Sinatra. We called him 'the Voice.'"

I wanted to be sitting with her in her old brownstone in Brooklyn. Dear would be there. She would pull the blackout curtains shut. I would tell them how the war would end and that no bombs would ever fall on Brooklyn. I would sit beside her and listen to Frank Sinatra. I would call him "the Voice."

"Blackout curtains can't stop radiation," Davis said. "They're no use."

"Davis," I said to him.

For a moment, my mother looked at Davis in silence, as if she had no idea what he was talking about.

"Maybe we should stay at school when the bomb falls," Davis said.

"All right," our father told him, "that's enough. That's enough about Civil Defense." Then he turned to our mother. "The school wants them to know what to do if a bomb should fall," he explained, "so they'll feel safe."

51

She shut her eyes. "So *that's* the plan," she said quietly. "And where will you be? I'd like to know *who* is going to be safe. I'd like to know *how* . . ."

"Maria," our father said. "Maria, don't . . ."

But it was too late. She stood up, crying, and turned to leave the room.

He got up to follow. At the dining room doorway, he stopped. "You should be doing your eye exercises," he told Davis.

As for me: I didn't know what to do. I slowly cleared the table and stacked the dishes in the sink.

Then I went down to the basement and sat within the shelter's masking-tape lines. We will come here after the bomb falls, I thought. We'll open a can of beef stew and heat it over Sterno. We'll heat it over Sterno and serve it on paper plates. "I'm sorry," Mom will say, "that we have to eat off paper plates. When I was a girl, we had Limoges." But it will be all right, I thought, to eat off paper plates. After dinner, we will play Parcheesi.

Davis came downstairs with his 3-D cards. He sat beside me, studying the cards, moving them back and forth in front of his face.

"Do you know the hot-water heater holds forty gallons?" I asked him. "Forty gallons would last us exactly twenty days."

I heard my father upstairs go into the living room and switch on the TV. I went upstairs and out to the backyard. I looked up at my mother's window.

It was eight o'clock. It was getting dark. My mother had turned on a light and shut her blinds.

When it is summer, I thought, I will be able to stand here and see shooting stars. I thought of Mrs. Harrison, my fifth-grade teacher, asking the class if we thought the night sky was lovelier if we could see a dozen brightly colored planets every night, or if the lonely moon, waning and waxing all on its own, was the loveliest thing of all, because it was just one thing, set off by itself to admire.

I saw a book of matches my father had left on the back steps and put it in my pocket. I opened the door beneath the screened-in porch and went in on my knees through the crawl space. The crawl space smelled of creosote, which my father had painted on the exposed wood of the porch's foundation. In back, behind the lawn mower, was a musty towel in which Davis and I had hidden a box of sparklers left over from the Fourth of July.

Standing in the backyard, I lit a sparkler. "Look, Mom, look!" I cried. "Mom, come to your window!"

She opened her blinds and peered out from between the slats.

"I'm writing your name!" I said. "Can you see it?"

I drew the sparkler quickly through the dark. A trail of white smoke spelled *M-A-R-I-A*. But by the time I got to the last *A,* the *M* had vanished. The white smoke that spelled her name disintegrated as it rose.

I lit another sparkler. I drew it in a circle around what remained of her name, as though the white smoke of the drifting circle might contain her name forever, holding it securely in place.

THE DIARIST

Here's one thing I remember, from all the things I never wrote down in my diary the summer I was eleven, the summer before my father died:

I was standing at the kitchen window, watching my brother, Davis, help our father load our station wagon with the gear we'd need to bring along— fishing rods and tackle boxes, canned foods and cooking pots, butterfly nets and BB rifles—when we left the next morning for Lumber Run, Pennsylvania, population 231. Lumber Run was paradise, my father said.

In fact, although Lumber Run had once been a boomtown, back when it still served the logging trains that once ran through there, from Williamsport to Wellsboro, it was now little more than a crossroads on Rt. 414, marked only by a general store, an abandoned Quonset hut, and a tar-papered tavern called the Wagon Wheel. But for two weeks each August, our father rented us a place there, an old farmhouse a former army buddy owned, wedged between the railway tracks and the banks of Pine Creek, where he liked to

55

go fishing. He said Lumber Run reminded him of Bishop, the coal-mining town where he'd grown up, before his brakeman father was killed in a machine accident in a switching yard outside Altoona.

I knew I should have been helping my father, like Davis, as he packed our stuff into the storage space he'd created by folding down the station wagon's middle seat, so that everything was fitted neatly together. And I knew this: I didn't want to go to Lumber Run, not this time, now that I knew my mother wasn't coming with us as she always had before. She'd already left the previous morning on the train from Silver Spring, Maryland, where we lived, to New York City, where she was going to visit her sister, who still lived in their family brownstone in Brooklyn. It was the same trip she'd taken at least monthly the year her mother was dying.

I dreaded my mother's departures, those Friday afternoons I came home from school to find her in her bedroom, packing her monogrammed train case—"I like to travel light," she said. I sat on the edge of her bed as she packed, watching her reflection in the small mirror secured to the satiny lining of the train case lid; together, we seemed one instrument, the mirror and I, catching the bright flutter of my mother's dress as she crossed the bedroom, back and forth, from her dresser to her closet to her vanity.

But this time she had packed the matching

Samsonites she'd bought at Woodward & Lothrop a few weeks before—a splurge from her inheritance, she said. From where I stood in her doorway, I could see that she wasn't traveling light. She asked if I'd please set her hatbox by the front door so she wouldn't forget it when the taxi came to take her to the station.

"I want to come with you," I told her.

She kept on packing as if she hadn't heard me.

"I've gone with you before," I urged. It was true. Once she had taken me with her for the weekend. We'd seen the Rockettes at Radio City Music Hall, and afterward we'd eaten at Schrafft's. "We'll be having the chicken à la king," she'd instructed the waitress without even consulting her menu. This proved she had once lived in New York City.

For a moment, she looked up. "No," she said. "You have to go with your father. He and I have already discussed that."

Then she resumed her work, folding her blouses into a suitcase, separating each layer with a sheet of white tissue.

At what point did I begin lying to my father, stammering nervous answers to whatever questions he asked me? "What are you doing?" he asked when he came in from packing the car to find me still standing in the kitchen.

"Making sandwiches," I told him. As I spoke, I wondered if he believed me, since he could see for himself I hadn't done anything, at least not yet—I hadn't even taken the bread from the refrigerator. My mother had always made our sandwiches for car trips; she liked to cut them into quarters before wrapping them in waxed paper.

"I want you to go to Wheaton Plaza with Davis," he told me. He said he was giving us each an extra buck so we could stock up on candy for the car ride.

Davis was waiting for me on the front stoop, holding the zippered change purse in which he stored his allowance. We headed for the plaza, through the woods behind the elementary school and across the divided highway. On the way, Davis told me our father had promised him he could sit in the front seat and navigate the whole way to Lumber Run.

"I don't believe you," I said.

"It's true," Davis answered.

When we got to Wheaton Plaza, we decided to separate, as we usually did. He went to Kahan's Hobby Shop to look at model cars; I went to S. S. Kresge to browse the bargain bins, where I sometimes found things, like scented bath salts or clip-on daisy earrings, that I could present to my mother.

It was there, standing near the bargain bins, that I first noticed the diary. It was bright pink and beautiful.

I lifted it from the rack to examine it. On its

laminated cover, a teenage girl with a ponytail was lying on her back with her legs upraised, as if she were admiring the way she had her ankles crossed, while chatting on her blue Princess phone. She was wearing capri pants with a matching top. But because the picture included neither the bed she was supposedly lying on nor the wall on which her feet were supposedly propped, she appeared to be floating in space, in defiance of all gravity. I knew right then that I had to make it mine.

"That's a *girl's* diary," Davis said when he joined me at the S. S. Kresge lunch counter, where we'd agreed to meet, and where, having already ordered a glass of ice water, I now sat daubing a moistened paper napkin on the sticky blemish the price tag had left on the diary's plasticized cover. Having just spent ten minutes negotiating my purchase—lifting the diary casually from its display rack and saying loudly to no one in particular, "I'll bet my sister will *love* this," then presenting it to the cashier and asking if it could be gift wrapped—I was still rocketing through the ionosphere of my anxiety, light-headed from the deoxygenated air.

But when Davis sat down, I felt something heavy and immutable settling beside me. I dropped the diary back into its paper sack and heard it land with a heavy thump, as if its cover girl had herself just fallen from orbit.

"It's the only kind they've got," I told him.

I couldn't tell if Davis had figured out that I was

lying. I started to add that Mrs. Tucker, my sixth-grade teacher, had once advised our class that we should all keep diaries, especially now that we were entering junior high, so we could look back one day at all the interesting things that happened in our lives. But as soon as I started to say this, I regretted it, remembering how my father had once told me that it was easy to spot a liar, because a liar always said more than he needed to.

"Sure," Davis said. "Like you've got something to write about."

I didn't know what to say. It was true I seldom had the urge to write things down, except occasionally, when I was angry. Once I had scrawled "I HATE DAVIS" on the notepad my mother kept by the kitchen phone, though as soon as I realized that my parents would see it, I tore off the top page and ripped it into shreds, so that all that remained was the clean white page beneath, on which my secret words were still almost invisibly imprinted.

Walking back from Wheaton Plaza, I tried to think of a way to make Davis promise not to tell about the diary; I considered telling him our parents had confided in me that they were worried about the bad grades he kept getting in school—maybe that would shut him up. But when we got to our block, I realized I should be worrying even more about what I'd say to my father if he asked to see what was inside the paper bag I was carrying. All summer he'd been telling me that I needed to stop playing so much with the neighborhood girls, and once, when he overheard me gossiping on the extension phone with my best friend, Denny, he warned me, "You don't need to be a Chatty Cathy."

But I was in luck. As we got close to our house, I saw my father standing in our backyard, talking to a next-door neighbor. I went to my room and stashed the diary in my duffel bag, tucking it beneath my shorts and T-shirts. All night, I thought of it there, secured in its dark enclosure, while I lay awake, trying to imagine what I'd soon be writing on its lined pages. I tried for a long time; but I kept thinking instead of the diary my mother had kept in high school, the one she sometimes shared with me on rainy afternoons, lifting it carefully from the bottom drawer of her dresser, a small book bound in red tooled leather, with the word DIARY filigreed in gold on its cover. It was made in Morocco, she'd once told me.

"Read to me," I asked her as she thumbed through the diary's fragile onionskin pages, pausing occasionally to read a passage aloud. In one entry, she recounted a date with a boy from Brooklyn Prep with whom she'd seen *Their Own Desire* with Norma Shearer; in another, she described her evening at the Emerald Ball in the Grand Ballroom of the Waldorf-Astoria, hosted by the Diocese of Brooklyn. She hadn't even made it across the Waldorf's lobby, she noted, before a half-dozen suitors had filled her dance card. She had worn a polished satin gown, pale yellow, with an Empire waist.

The next day, Davis and I took turns as navigators, with one of us sitting in the front seat beside our father while the other sat in the rear. I sat in front first, plotting our route from home to Harrisburg, where we crossed the Susquehanna. The whole way, my father kept inventing games for him and me to play, like the one where we tried to tell which drivers were Catholics, like we were, by checking whether or not they had rosaries hanging from their rearview mirrors or plastic Virgins mounted on their dashboards, as we did. When we passed Burma Shave signs posted along the highway, we read them aloud together: NO LADY LIKES / TO DANCE OR DINE / ACCOMPANIED BY / A PORCUPINE / BURMA SHAVE / BURMA SHAVE. I knew even then, I suppose, that I belonged to my mother, just as Davis was our father's, but that morning, riding in the car beside him, I could remember times when I'd belonged to my father, too, sitting with him in the bathtub as a small child, while he rinsed my back with warm, soapy water, or leaning against him on the sofa on Saturday nights, watching *Have Gun, Will Travel*.

After lunch, Davis and I changed places. I sat in back, listening to my father play the same games with Davis he'd just played with me. After a while, I shut my eyes and tried to imagine what my mother was doing—perhaps she was sitting at the kitchen table in Brooklyn at that very moment, I thought, drinking sugared coffee with her sister. As soon as I pictured it, it seemed like something I might want to set down in my diary, although written from the perspective of my sitting at the table with them.

When I opened my eyes, I saw that we were passing through Sunbury, where we'd stopped the previous summer, at my insistence, to visit a snake farm I'd seen touted for miles on garish billboards. But as soon as the guide had shown us the first chicken-wire cage of timber rattlers massed horribly together, I'd gotten sick and had been forced to wait with my mother in the gift shop, looking at miniature souvenir teacups, while Davis completed the tour with our father.

After Sunbury, the road narrowed and the small towns grew smaller yet. I knelt on the backseat, looking out the rear window, so that I saw the names of towns only after we passed through them, catching sight of signs meant to welcome arriving travelers—Dewart, Duboistown, Larryville, Avis. All afternoon, we drove deeper and deeper into my father's world, through quick tableaux of thick-waisted women draping their laundry on porch rails and teenagers huddling on the roadsides, tossing rocks at telephone poles. I'd been to places like these, the times my father took us to Bishop, where his sister still lived with her husband on a truck farm at the edge of town, past the coal mines. To get there, we had to drive by the boney dumps,

63

the worthless mounds of slate and low-grade coal that the mining companies had rejected as waste. People said the boney dumps were dangerous; they could combust from compression. If even a small fire went unseen in a mound of boney, my aunt once told me, the whole thing could explode without warning.

It was after dark when we got to Lumber Run. Our father trained the station wagon's high beams on the house so he could find his way across the front porch to undo the padlock that secured the door. Then Davis and I dragged our suitcases from the car to our rooms. "I'll heat a few cans of ravioli," our father told us.

My room was the smallest in the house, tucked behind the kitchen. I'd chosen it the first time we'd come to Lumber Run because my mother had told me it reminded her of the butler's pantry where she'd played dolls as a small girl in her family's house in Brooklyn—not that *this* little house ever needed a *butler*, she added. But I had always liked my room, at least until now, with its austere furnishings and theatrical severity; I'd liked lying on the narrow bed in the late afternoons, with the door closed, studying the battered fiber-board dresser and the single small window whose green paper shade snapped up violently when touched. Sometimes I'd pretend I was staying in a room in a run-down boardinghouse or fleabag hotel, like the ones I'd seen in western movies. But now, as I stood there, picking at the flecks of ceiling plaster that had fallen onto the bedspread over the winter, the room seemed merely grim. It was nothing like my room at home, a room I'd taken to redecorating almost monthly, setting a kerosene lamp on my study desk to create a colonial effect, or hanging wooden wind chimes from the ceiling light to make the room look Japanese. This room would bear no changes; this was a room that was meant to change me.

I opened my suitcase and pulled the diary from beneath my shorts and T-shirts; then I sat down on the bed, holding it in my lap. For a while, I just stared at it, as if I were somehow expecting it to speak, although that was really stupid—I knew that. It was a diary; I was supposed to be speaking to it. But I could feel a muteness settling in my throat, as if something mangled were lodged there, and the longer I studied the diary, the more I could see how cheap it really looked, at least beneath the harsh, naked bulb of the ceiling light. For the first time, I saw how a few pages were already coming unglued from its binding, and how a crease had begun to deform its flimsy, plasticized cover. Even the cover girl looked sort of pathetic, now that I could see that the yellow of her ponytail had been printed somewhat out of register. It's not *my* fault, I wanted suddenly to explain to someone—it was the room's fault, or my father's, or my mother's, for not coming with us. Right then, I hated the diary. I wanted to hurl it to the floor and step on it.

"Time for supper!" I heard my father call out.

When I came into the kitchen, I saw that he looked happy, spooning ravioli onto paper plates. He was humming along to some song playing on the transistor radio propped on the windowsill.

"Hungry enough to eat a horse?" he asked me.

Then Davis came in and joined us. As we ate, our father kept telling us how he'd soon be catching plenty of blue trout for our suppers. "Me, too," Davis told him.

I was silent: It felt wrong, sitting there beside the empty seat that belonged to my mother. I wondered if maybe she was having her supper then, too, or if maybe she'd gone someplace, like to a movie with her sister. As I imagined my mother, I began feeling bad about having wanted to hurt my own diary.

As soon as my father finished his meal, he carried his paper plate across the kitchen and stuffed it into the garbage. "Let's have some fun," he said.

"Like what?" Davis asked.

I looked at my father. I thought maybe he wanted to take us to the Wagon Wheel—he and our mother had often liked going there at night to drink beer, the two of them sitting on stools at the pine-paneled bar while Davis and I fed nickels to the jukebox, playing "The Wayward Wind" over and over, because our mother said she liked it. Or maybe he just wanted to take us out back to practice shooting tin cans with our Daisy BB rifles, as he'd taught us on a weekend camping trip a few months before. He'd gotten us the rifles for Christmas.

"I thought we'd head down to the railroad tracks," he said.

I liked walking to the tracks with my father. More than once he'd told Davis and me the tracks made him think of his father, who must have passed through Lumber Run at least a few times, or so he imagined, on freights hauling coal.

Davis and I went to change into our sneakers, then joined our father in the backyard, where he was waiting with his flashlight. We followed him across the cut grass and through a small arcade of trees, toward the watchman's shanty, where highway crews stored salt for winter roads, now that trains no longer stopped there.

"Quiet," he said when we got to the railway crossing. He bent down toward the tracks, as he did each time he brought us here, pretending to be listening for the distant sound of the freight train on which his father had long ago ridden.

"Can you hear it?" he asked.

Davis and I just stood there in silence, watching him. Nothing was coming. For a moment, I tried to imagine my father as he must have been as a boy growing up in Bishop, though it was hard to do so, since he spoke so seldom of his childhood, except to say he'd had to go to work when he was ten, sweeping out railway cars, and that when he was twelve, he'd been consigned for a year to the State Youth Sanatorium for Tuberculosis.

Once he had told us that when he was a small boy his father had called him "honey."

He stepped into the railway bed, almost slipping on the oily gravel. Davis and I moved toward him. I couldn't believe how dark it was, though when I looked up I saw the Dog Star quietly blazing above us. "It's called Sirius," my mother once told me when we were sitting together in our backyard on a summer night a few years before.

"Here you go," our father said as he reached into one of his trouser pockets. He withdrew a fistful of coins, from which he counted out the pennies. Then Davis and I laid the pennies on the tracks, one by one, knowing that when we returned the next morning, we'd find them flattened and flung into the high weeds by night trains we'd neither seen nor heard as we slept.

The next morning, I watched my father head down the narrow path to Pine Creek, his fishing rod and tackle box in one hand, his creel slung over his shoulder, beating on his back as he walked. I was sitting on the front steps, eating my cereal.

"Don't you want to come?" he'd asked as he was leaving.

"Not right now," I'd told him. I'd said I'd try to catch up later, after I'd done the dishes.

I watched him walk away until he disappeared behind a stand of cattails; then I carried my bowl back to the house. I was relieved not to have gone with him to Pine Creek, where he would have once again instructed me how best to bait my hook. I hated touching the worms, with their greasy, quivering bodies, as I pulled them from the bait bucket, and I hated jabbing them onto the barbed hooks, making sure I'd stuck each of them onto the hook in at least two places so it wouldn't fall off too quickly in the water.

The house was silent when I entered it. Davis had left earlier that morning; I didn't know where he'd gone. But that was all right. I liked being alone with no one around to see me. The whole past year, I'd begun feigning illness on school days so I could stay home by myself. Once my parents left for work, I'd lie for hours on the basement sofa, slowly devouring the coffee cakes I made for myself from Bisquik, brown sugar, and margarine, until I could feel myself at long last dissolving—nameless, benumbed, unfettered—into the noise and canned laughter of the game shows I watched on TV.

But now I had something important to do. I went into my room and retrieved the diary from the drawer where I'd hidden it the night before. I was glad to see it looked a lot better by daylight; even the cover girl looked brighter and more cheerful. I carried it out to the front porch glider, along with a pencil I'd found in a kitchen drawer. If someone showed up, I figured, I could slip it quickly beneath a cushion.

But when I sat down and opened the diary—I

was ready to inscribe my first entry—I was jarred by the emptiness of its white ruled pages. What was I supposed to write there? The only thing I could think of was the odd, throbbing absence of my mother, and how the previous summer I'd sat beside her on the very same glider, reading the *Reader's Digest* condensed books I'd found in the attic, while she flipped through back issues of fashion magazines, occasionally pausing to comment on a pair of shoes or a cocktail dress she particularly admired. But that wasn't something I could put in my diary. What would be the point of that? It was stupid—*case closed*.

Maybe if I just got a bite to eat, I thought, I might calm down. I went inside to get a piece of bread from the loaf I'd seen on the kitchen counter. I ate the bread quickly, standing there; then I ate another slice, and then another, and then another one yet. Then I saw how much bread I had eaten and worried that my father would be upset with me for eating so much, but that didn't stop me—I couldn't seem to help myself. I laid a slice on the counter and rolled it around until it turned back into dough, and then I ate that, too, because it was sweeter like that, almost like candy.

By the time I got back to the porch glider, I felt sluggish. I told myself I should lie down, since I felt too tired to write, even though I could feel something hard and insistent tugging inside me, telling me I should try to put at least something on paper, even if it was something I invented, since

I wasn't sure I could think of anything true to say. I opened the diary to try again, but I felt worse, just from holding it. I worried that I'd thrown away my money by buying it. Maybe I'd made a terrible mistake. What if I needed my money for something else?

That's when I heard Davis come into the house through the back door, laughing and talking with someone whose voice I didn't recognize. I shoved the diary beneath one of the glider cushions, then went into the house.

"Dad's looking for you," Davis said when I came into the kitchen, where he was standing with his friend Frank, a local boy he'd met while fishing the previous summer. After their initial meeting, they'd gone out hiking together almost every afternoon, canteens strapped to their army surplus belts, while I went to country auctions in the car with my mother, who was trying to add to her collection of cut glass.

I could see Frank didn't much like me—or maybe he was just shy, as I'd once heard Davis telling our father. In any case, Frank barely looked in my direction as Davis told me all about the morning they'd spent together—how they'd gone to the tracks to gather the flattened pennies, as he and I had planned to do, and how they had walked to the remains of the old sawmill with BB rifles to shoot at some black snakes Frank's brother said he had seen there. Now they were packing a bag lunch, Davis said, to bring to our father.

I didn't need to ask if the BB rifle Frank had used had in fact been mine; I could see it sitting right there in the corner, propped against the wall.

"See you," Frank murmured in my direction as they left.

I was alone again, and I wasn't sure what to do with myself. I didn't want to resume my diary. I didn't want to read a book. There was nothing good to eat in the house except the loaf of bread, from which I'd already eaten too much. For a moment, I was sorry they hadn't asked me to come with them.

That's when I decided to follow them down the path toward Pine Creek. At first, I couldn't hear them ahead of me, not even when I stopped in the first clearing in the cattails, where people sometimes dumped old tires. But by the time I got to the second clearing—someone had abandoned an old car there, I noticed, a broken-down junker with its running boards nearly rusted out—I could hear them laughing. I stepped into the cattails. From there, I could see them sitting side by side at the edge of Pine Creek, talking back and forth between themselves as they took off their shoes and socks and rolled up the legs of their blue jeans. They stepped into the water—neither seemed shocked by its sudden coldness—and began wading toward the rock where our father sat fishing.

Then I saw Davis start to slip on the creek's mossy stone bottom. I could see small whirlpools of white water clutching at his ankles, and a look of panic rising in his face. I wondered if Frank could see the panic, too.

For a moment, I thought to call out to warn my brother, suddenly remembering the times he and I had played there together, building small dams from branches and twigs and then coming back later to kick them apart.

But I stayed silent.

Davis slipped; Frank caught him. Frank laughed, and Davis splashed him with water. Then they continued wading toward our father, Davis holding the paper lunch sack above his head, the way a soldier carries his rifle through high water.

I stepped forward from the edge of the cattails. But when I emerged into the open, I saw that my father was watching me.

He waved. I waved, my hand stirring from the cattails a sudden updraft made visible by gnats. But I went no farther. I wasn't sure if I was waving hello or good-bye.

What might I have written about my father in my diary, had I been able to write down anything at all? That I felt afraid when he watched me too long or too closely? Or that the things he kept warning me to stop doing, like cutting out Winnie Winkle fashion paper dolls from the Sunday funnies or designing elaborate ball gowns for my favorite movie stars, were in fact the very things that came most naturally, unbidden, from my hand? *If thy right hand offend thee, cut it off.* Or maybe I would have simply written that I loved him, and missed him, and that I wanted him to call me "honey," too, as his father had called him.

In any case, I was unable to write even a word. Not one word the whole time.

Each morning for the next three days, as soon as I was alone in the house, I resumed my seat on the porch glider, my pencil poised, my diary opened on my lap, waiting for words to strike. One morning it occurred to me that I could address the whole diary to my mother, making her a chronicle of all the things I'd done since I'd last seen her, though in my heart I knew I'd done nothing worth writing down. Another time, I decided I should save the diary to use later, after I'd begun what I hoped would one day become my real life, a life just like the one my mother described herself as once having had, catching a taxi to the Stork Club for cocktails before grabbing a late supper at Luchow's or Toots Shor's.

But for the most part, I just sat there until I felt too lonely to persist. Then I wandered over to the general store to buy red licorice and pretzel rods, counting and recounting my coins, worried that I was depleting my savings too quickly; or I walked the railroad tracks across the old wooden trestle, staring down into the depths below, which I could see through gaps in the cross ties. I carried the diary with me, tucked into my waistband and covered by my camp shirt. But the diary some-times chafed me as I walked, and when this happened, I'd be seized by a sudden desire to throw it onto the tracks, even though that desire flooded me with shame, as if I'd just caught myself wanting to kill something small and defenseless. Once, on my way home from one of my walks, I ran into Mrs. Purvis, a widow I'd met with my mother at an auction the previous summer. She invited me back to her house, where we sat on her porch, drinking sweet tea while she showed me an old scrapbook filled with photos of her and her dead husband. When I stood to leave, I decided I wanted to show her the diary, though I told her I'd just found it on the side of the road. "I don't know," she said as she examined it. "It looks mighty new to me."

As for my father: I knew he was upset with me. Each late afternoon when he got home from fishing, he came to my room and stood in the doorway as if there was something he wanted to say. But I just kept on reading, stretched out on the bed, its coarse woolen blanket tucked tight into army corners, as he had taught me. After he turned and walked away, I shut the book and listened to him as he crossed the kitchen to the sink. I could hear him turn on the tap, and I could hear the water rushing forward as he began to gut and clean whatever fish he'd caught that day.

But on the fourth afternoon, he got angry.

When I got home from walking the railroad tracks,

I found him in the backyard, watering the lawn with a garden hose, as he sometimes did, so that he could come back later and hunt for night crawlers, which emerged when the soil was wet.

"I want you to tell me what's going on," he said as soon as he saw me.

"What do you mean?" I asked, worried that he'd somehow found the diary, even though I felt sure I had it with me, tucked into my waistband. I had to fight the urge to reassure myself by touching it.

"You haven't come fishing like I've asked," he said, looking at me directly.

"But I'm going to," I told him.

"Sure," he said. "When?"

"I will."

"So you say," he said.

I just stood there, shifting from foot to foot. Had he been like my mother, I might have distracted him by getting him to tell me some story about himself, but that didn't work with him.

Later, at supper, Davis started talking about an abandoned CCC camp he'd come across while hiking up a fire trail with Frank; they'd seen the remains of a few barracks and a tree growing through what they figured had once been the floor of the mess hall. Our father said the whole country should still be thanking FDR for the CCC and the New Deal, because without him no one would have gotten even an honest dollar for an honest day's work.

As soon as I had finished eating, I excused myself. I couldn't stop thinking about my diary. Even though I knew I'd returned it to its drawer the second I'd gotten back into the house, I needed to check to make sure it was there, the same way my mother sometimes had to turn the car around and drive home, worried that she'd left a cigarette burning and that it had already fallen onto the carpet.

But I was also nervous about being seen returning to my bedroom, since I didn't want to do anything that would call attention to myself. So I went out back to catch lightning bugs, just like normal. A few minutes later, Davis came out of the kitchen door and settled himself in a chair beneath the back porch light, looking through a copy of *Boys' Life* he'd gotten from Frank. He and Frank liked reading *Boys' Life* together, mesmerizing themselves with stories of scouts who proved quick-minded in the midst of disaster, slashing open a snakebite puncture on a child's arm to suck the venom out or forming a human chain to rescue a skater who'd fallen through thin ice.

I liked catching lightning bugs; I liked collecting them in jars with lids I'd studded with air holes. At night, the jars made small, radiant galaxies that by morning would be dead.

I went to the honeysuckle bushes in the side yard, where the lightning bugs were flickering among the fragrant white and yellow flowers; I reached out a hand and grabbed one from where it hovered, flashing, in midair. Then I remembered a trick a girl had once told me about in school. If you pulled off a lightning bug's belly, she said, and stuck it on your finger, you could make a ring from it, because when a lightning bug died, its belly continued to glow.

I wasn't sure I could actually do it, but I gave it my full attention, first pulling the wings from the lightning bug's body, then setting its belly, still glowing, on my left ring finger. If I squinted, I realized, the lightning bug's luminescent belly looked almost like the yellow diamond solitaire my mother had inherited after her mother's death. But who would inherit the solitaire, I wondered, when my mother died? It would never go to a boy.

I looked up and saw Davis still reading beneath the porch light. I walked across the yard toward him, holding out my left hand as steady as possible.

"Look," I said, showing him what I had made.

He looked up briefly from his magazine and gazed at my finger. "That's dumb," he said.

"No," I said. "It's beautiful."

Then I heard the screen door slam, and when I looked up, I saw my father coming out to the porch from the kitchen. I hurriedly turned my hand over, and the firefly's belly dropped into the grass. For a moment, I watched as it extinguished itself like a cigarette butt's dying ember.

"What are you doing?" my father asked.

"Getting the lightning bugs something to eat," I told him. To prove it, I bent over and yanked up a few handfuls of grass to stuff into one of the jars.

"I thought maybe you boys were telling ghost stories," he said. "That's what my brothers and I used to do after dark. Did you ever hear 'The Monkey's Paw'? We always liked 'The Monkey's Paw.'"

"We saw it on TV," I told him.

"Oh," he said. Then he stepped forward from the porch into the dark. "I want you boys to help me look for night crawlers," he told us.

He instructed Davis to go around to the front porch and fetch a few flashlights and the dirt-filled coffee can in which he kept his live bait. When Davis left, he turned toward me. "Maybe you won't mind helping with *this*," he said. "Since you can't seem to find it within yourself to come fishing, I mean."

"I want to help," I told him, though it wasn't true. I hated searching for night crawlers. I hated having to grasp them, damp and slick, as they first emerged from the ground, and I hated the way they tore into pieces if I got nervous and pulled at them too hard or quickly.

Davis came back around the side of the house, carrying the bait can, along with two flashlights, which he was toting in his pant pockets. He had switched on a third flashlight and was holding it under his chin as he walked, so that his illuminated face looked cadaverous and ghoulish. "Oooohh," he was moaning like a ghost as he came toward us, "you've got three wishes on the monkey's paw . . ."

"Okay, that's enough," our father said. "Let's get down to business."

For a moment, I stood there without moving, as if Davis's words had cast some spell that had stilled me. I knew what my wish would be, if one wish were granted me: *Please let me seem, even if only for this hour, my father's son.* I knew the time had come. I knew I had to please him.

Then I heard my own voice speaking, a muffled sound, as if from a distance: "Dad," I was saying, "I'll go search in the compost."

I could see my father was surprised by what I'd said, just as I was. He knew I was afraid of the compost pile. It sat in the darkest and farthest part of the yard, near the stand of trees that separated our house from the Wagon Wheel's parking lot. Davis and Frank had once told me that rats went to feed there, drawn by the stench of decomposition; they said brown snakes liked to nest there, seeking the warmth that rises from decay. But it was also where night crawlers were most abundant. I knew that.

"Are you sure?" my father asked.

"It's not fair," Davis complained. "Dad said he wanted us to do this *together.*"

"Yes, I'm sure," I told my father.

"All right," he said.

He handed me a flashlight and I started to walk away.

"Wait," he said. He removed his fishing cap, the one to which he affixed his hand-tied flies, and set it on my head. "Walk softly," he told me. "Keep your eyes peeled."

I crossed the yard, walking softly. I kept my eyes peeled.

When I got to the compost, I stepped over the low chicken-wire fencing that enclosed it, sinking to my ankles in the soft mulch. I guided my flashlight's beam back and forth across the surface. Everywhere the light fell, I saw small, sudden motions: a wood spider struggling through the sticky albumen glazing an eggshell; pale grubs devouring wet leaves. Then I heard music, the faint sound of a song playing on the jukebox at the Wagon Wheel. It was hard not to think of my mother, to picture her sitting at the bar in her white sun-dress with the spaghetti straps, holding her beer glass aloft. "Meet my pretty wife," my father always said as he introduced her to his fisherman friends—"Meet my wife, pretty Maria."

I looked up. On the other side of the yard, my father was holding a flashlight for Davis, who was kneeling within the wide circumference of its beam. Davis was lowering his hand toward the ground and pulling up a night crawler.

I wanted my father to watch me. I knelt in the compost and reached down, and all at once I saw at least a dozen night crawlers emerging simultaneously from their air holes, as if in response to a single command. I was just beginning to touch one, preparing to yank it out from its hole, when suddenly something fell toward me—a leaf?—and landed on my shoulder.

I turned to look: Its wings struck my face. Whatever it was, it was caught in the fabric of my shirt, straining to pull itself free. It jerked upward and rose briefly, only to catch itself again on my collar. I could feel the violence and terror of its movement at my throat, thrashing and thrashing.

"Get it off me!" I cried.

My father came running, his flashlight's beam swinging crazily through the dark, like an emergency.

"Get it off me!" I begged him. "Get it off!"

He pointed the flashlight at my collar, where the creature was struggling, its pale green wings furiously beating.

Through the flashlight's beam, I could see my father study me. I saw how I looked in his eyes.

"It's a luna moth," he said. He reached toward my collar and flicked it with his fingertips. Suddenly it seemed small and insufficient. It rose and flew away.

"I thought you'd been bitten by a snake," he said.

"Me, too," I said. "That's what I thought, too." We both knew I was lying.

"Just get inside," he muttered.

I switched off my flashlight and walked back

across the yard. As I passed Davis, he whispered dramatically, "Oooohh, it's the curse of the monkey's paw . . ."

I said nothing back. When I got to the porch, I didn't turn around to look at my father.

I simply opened the back door and stepped into the kitchen, flinching from the sudden brightness of the ceiling light. When my eyes adjusted, I saw it. I saw it lying right there on the kitchen table. My diary. Someone had found it and taken it from my dresser, and now it was lying there, just lying there, out in the open, beside the salt and pepper shakers.

That night, I didn't claim the diary by taking it back to my room; in fact, I didn't even want to touch it. I went right to bed and stayed there until late the next morning, when I heard my father drive off in the station wagon, headed to Slate Run, where he was planning to try his hand at fly-fishing with some men he'd met at the Wagon Wheel.

When I got up for breakfast, the diary was still sitting in the center of the table. I just sat there looking at it as I ate my cereal, imagining the things I might have written down had I gone to New York with my mother. Perhaps we would have had dinner at Michel's, my mother's favorite restaurant in Park Slope, or perhaps we would have taken in an early movie at the Rialto. Perhaps I would have been happy simply to sit in the

Victorian room my grandmother had called her "boudoir," remembering the time she had invited me in to ask me questions for a personality quiz she'd prepared on a legal pad especially for me. "Whom do you prefer," she had asked, "Jayne Mansfield or Marilyn Monroe? Whom do you regard as the greater actress, Bette Davis or Greta Garbo? Which do you prefer, the plain Hershey bar or the Hershey with almonds?"

I sat at the kitchen table most of the morning, as if I were bidding the diary adieu. But I couldn't sit there forever. I had something to do, something I had figured out the night before while lying awake in my room.

I waited until I finished lunch. Then I stacked my dishes in the sink and went to the broom closet, where my father stored our Daisy BB rifles, out of immediate reach. I took my rifle and carried it out to the front porch glider. Then I began to clean it, just as my father had taught me, first moistening a cleaning patch with a few drops of heavy oil, then inserting the patch directly into the muzzle on a long rod in order to swab the bore. When I was done, I opened the small paper cylinder of BBs and poured them into my palm; I fed the BBs slowly into the narrow loading tube affixed to the base of the barrel.

I carried the loaded rifle down the path toward Pine Creek, past the first clearing and through the cattails. At the second clearing, I stopped. I pulled hard on the cocking lever and raised the rifle straight, positioning the old junked car in its sight.

I fired. The first shot struck the junker's windshield. I pressed the trigger again so that a second shot struck the glass, and when I saw that my aim was right and good, I pulled the trigger over and over, until the windshield cracked into a silvery web and then shattered, raining small bits of glass across the dashboard. I liked the way it felt. I walked around to the driver's side and shot out those windows, too, and then I shot at the side panel until it was scored and dimpled, and then I walked around to the other side and did the whole thing over again. Finally, I took aim at the small winged ornament on the rusty hood. But I wasn't through.

I set the rifle down and walked back to the house empty-handed. Once there, I took the diary from the kitchen table and carried it back down to the clearing. I opened one of the car doors, set the diary on the front seat, and then backed up until I had the cover girl within my rifle's sight. I fired at her, too, again and again, until she and the diary were both obliterated, the pink plastic cover split from its cardboard backing, the blank pages shredded.

Later, I ate supper with Davis. We'd heated up a few more cans of ravioli, since our father had warned us he'd be late—he was stopping at the Wagon Wheel to drink some beer with his buddies. After supper, I went into the front room to wait on the musty horsehair sofa. I was eager to tell my father how I had practiced my marksmanship, as he had encouraged.

I heard him on the porch before he came in. From the way he grabbed at the screen door, I could tell he was angry. "Where are you?" he called out as he came into the house. He was calling my name.

I was scared. The room was dark. It was late. "I'm here," I finally said.

Suddenly my father was standing in the doorway. "What the hell did you think you were doing?" he demanded. "What the hell made you think you could destroy something that isn't even yours?"

I knew what I thought I was doing: I was trying to please him. Even now, looking back, I honestly believe that. But what could I have said to him then? That I had hoped to turn myself into a son he might love?

My silence made him angrier. "That damn car isn't yours!" he bellowed. He said the car belonged to one of the bartenders at the Wagon Wheel. It wasn't a junker. It ran just fine. He said he was just drinking a beer and minding his own damn business, when some man he'd never even met before came into the bar and told him what I had done, how I'd been down at the creek shooting at a car until I'd destroyed it. "And just how the hell do you think you're going to pay that back?" he shouted.

I could see that he was trying to contain himself,

even though he was furious. I just listened to him yell. After a while, he started to spend himself until, finally, he just stood there in silence. It wasn't until then that he noticed that the room he was standing in was dark. He reached over and switched on the table lamp.

"Do you have anything to say for yourself?" he asked.

"No," I said.

"Then I want you to get ready for bed," he said. "I'll go ahead and check you."

I knew what he meant: Each night in Lumber Run before Davis and I went to bed, we stood before him so he could check our bodies for ticks that we ourselves might not have spotted.

He unscrewed the shade from the table lamp next to the sofa and bent my head into the arc of light, parting my hair with his fingers as he inspected my scalp.

"Stand up," he said.

I stood. I began to undress, as I did each night: first my shoes and socks, then my pants, then my shirt, until I was standing there naked. He lifted the table lamp and moved it slowly back and forth across my body, studying my chest, my back, my buttocks, my legs. I felt right then as if there were nothing about me that was not visible to him. I could feel the heat of the bulb on my skin.

I hate you, I thought. *I hate you, I hate you.*

In retrospect, I'm not sure who I was hating most right then, as I stood there—my father, my mother, or myself. That night I didn't know that my father would soon die suddenly of liver failure, or that it would be Davis who would one day explain to me that it was not he but Mrs. Purvis who had told my father that she had seen me with a diary, or that I had scarcely even begun what was to become my life of secrets.

I knew only the heat of the bulb as it passed over my naked body. *I hate you*, I thought, *I hate you*. I no longer had a diary. But for the first time I felt as if I actually needed one, a need that was at once acute and unfamiliar. It wasn't that I needed to speak to my mother in her absence; it wasn't that I wanted to make something up. For the first time, I wanted to write something down, something true, even if I had no idea what words I'd one day use in doing so.

SNAPSHOTS OF THE VISIBLE MAN

The Night He Died

The night my father died, the house was so hot that we propped box fans in our bedroom windows, then escaped to the backyard, where we sat at the wobbly picnic table the developer had given us, one free with each house sold.

"There's no breeze," Davis complained. He was twelve; I was eleven.

"Try this," our mother said, touching her sweaty tumbler of Tom Collins first to her right wrist, then to her left.

I touched my glass of iced tea to my wrist, and my pulse ached with vibrant numbness. "It helps," I told her.

Davis stood. He stepped onto the edge of our bench; as he did so, its opposite side, where I sat, rose like a seesaw. Then he hoisted himself into the willow tree. He began climbing—up through its slender branches, up through its dense curtain of leaves. He climbed higher and higher, and just before he disappeared from view, I thought of the

89

time he'd scaled the tree to hang bird feeders for our father, securing them with fishing line, then filling them with seed.

Our father had planted the willow himself, as a sapling, and later a Dutch elm, a hemlock pine, and a Tree of Heaven, knotting each with jute to its wooden stake, then wrapping it in gauze. Early Saturday mornings, I sometimes watched from my bedroom window as Davis helped him. Together they constructed trellises; they thrust posthole diggers down through hard soil, erecting a chain-link fence.

It seemed wrong not to want to help them; it seemed wrong to want to stay inside, waiting for my mother to wake up. By then, she had begun her insomniac nights, sitting up by herself on the screened-in porch and listening to her portable radio.

One Saturday morning she came to my room. She sat on the edge of my bed, holding the Japanese doll I kept on my nightstand. "I'm sorry," she said. "I'm all right. I'm fine."

She studied the doll's delicate white bisque hands. I looked back out the window to where my father and Davis were working.

She changed the subject. "I'll bet you're thinking how nice the yard looks," she said.

But I was trying to remember how the yard had looked before my father had devoted himself to its continual improvement, back when our house was new and the yard was nothing more than unsodded mud steadily eroding into the woods behind us. At that time, it had contained only the redwood picnic table, adrift beneath the clothesline.

Davis and I had played there, overturning the picnic table and pretending it was our life raft. Ten yards away, our house was the *Titanic*.

"Fire!" we called. "Fire!" We tried to summon our parents to their bedroom window, hoping they might raise their Venetian blind and find their two sons huddled on the upside-down table, clutching its overturned legs. But no matter how loudly we called, they never appeared there; nor did they appear among the other passengers, those whom we fantasized struggling against locked portholes or rushing to the upper decks, from which they hurled themselves—some were aflame, like human torches—into the icy Atlantic below.

"Don't look," I told Davis. Everywhere the water was littered with dead bodies: women in bloated evening gowns, men in seared tuxedoes, and sometimes, floating among them, their pajamaed children, lifelessly bobbing but holding hands. Throughout, the band played "Nearer My God to Thee."

Then the ship went down, smoldering in the muddy brown sea.

We were orphans.

But our danger wasn't over. We braced ourselves for the undertow.

"We're going to die!" Davis screamed, rocking the table from side to side, as if a rough wave were right then breaking beneath us, threatening to cast us overboard. I lay facedown on the redwood boards, clinging to their splintery edges.

Then Davis stopped the rocking. We turned around, away from the house, and we were safe on an open sea. We lay on our backs, murmuring the names of animals whose shapes appeared in the clouds above us; we sat cross-legged, eating the jelly sandwiches we'd brought along. We could float like that for hours, just the two of us, lazily waiting to be rescued.

"Hello, down there," Davis whispered from the willow tree. Each time he moved, its low branches trembled, brushing the tabletop.

I moved closer to my mother. She still wore the dress she'd worn that morning to the hospital, black polished cotton imprinted with gold coins; she still wore her lucky bracelet, silver dollars affixed to its chain. But already she seemed different, more somber and more still, as if something deep inside her had begun a steady metamorphosis that would one day render her empowered or reduced.

She was a widow.

She was tranquilized. At the Catholic hospital, a nun had given her an injection. Afterward, she sat for hours in the corridor, amid the gurneys and the carts, amid emergencies, holding the paper sack into which she'd packed my father's calfskin wallet, his wingtip shoes, his Hamilton watch.

"I'm sorry," I wanted to tell her. Her grief, like all of her emotions, seemed larger than us all.

She lit a Parliament.

"Your father has come home," she said. "He has come home to always watch over us."

For a long time, we sat in silence, watching a searchlight sweep the dark sky. It advertised the grand opening of Foxmoor, a new subdivision of split-levels.

Christmas Trees

"That's how I know my feelings are perfectly normal," my mother explained, recounting the things she'd heard that afternoon on a TV show; the topic had been "holiday depression." Now it was eight o'clock on Christmas Eve, and the three of us were standing at the Boys' Club Christmas tree lot, waiting for one of the volunteer salesmen to notice us. The salesmen were congregated by a tar-paper shack, warming their hands over a fire they'd built in an oil drum, like hoboes. A loudspeaker blared "The Little Drummer Boy."

"Maybe they don't know we need help," my mother said. She had begun searching in her handbag for a cigarette.

"You have to pick a tree," Davis told her.

"Don't tell her what to do," I said. I was in charge. So I could pay for the tree, my mother had slipped me five dollars, just as she always did in restaurants before the check came. She believed it was wrong for a woman to handle money when she was being escorted by a man.

93

"We're too late," Davis said. "They're not waiting on us because we're so late. I think they're closed."

But a salesman finally came toward us. I recognized him as someone who lived in the next subdivision, in a ranch house on Haywood Drive. I wondered how we must have appeared to him— our mother dressed in high heels and her coat with a fox collar; Davis and I in matching corduroy car coats, like old men. I wondered if he knew our father had died.

"We only want Scotch pine," I told him. In the car, we had discussed the fact that our father had always purchased Scotch pine.

"Maybe one of those will do," my mother said, pointing to a row of trees still bound with twine and propped against a snow fence. Earlier, while we'd been waiting, she had concluded that the unbound trees were probably worthless, having already been passed over by other customers.

We followed the salesman to the fence. He grabbed the biggest tree and cut its twine with a knife. Then he slipped on his leather gloves, grasped the tree by its trunk, and roughly shook it until its branches spread.

"That's it," I said. Suddenly I felt worried, for I'd forgotten we were supposed to inspect it for bare spots, as our father had always done.

"Yes, sir," the salesman told me. "That's it, all right. That's the tree you want."

It seemed we'd already bought it; now it was ours. The salesman helped us carry it to our car, the white

Impala convertible our mother had purchased with life insurance money.

When we saw that the tree was too big for the car's trunk, Davis and I wrapped it in a sheet while our mother put the top down.

The salesman helped us lift it into the backseat. It was heavy, like a body.

"You'll have to sit in back and hold it," I told Davis.

Then we climbed into the car and pulled off toward home, down Sligo Creek Parkway, and left onto Carroll Knolls Road. "A new car really makes a difference in how you feel," my mother said.

But I felt conspicuous riding through our subdivision like this, with the top down and the windows rolled up. On Homewood Parkway, a carload of teenagers waved as they passed us. I couldn't tell whether they were making fun of us or whether they thought our car was neat and hoped we'd wave back.

We stopped for the light. On the right was Connecticut Terrace, which my mother always called "the widows' apartments"—a small complex of prewar garden apartments with casement windows lined with snake plants, Hummel figurines, and Avon bottles filled with colored water.

"I hope I never have to live there," my mother said each time we passed by.

I fiddled with the dashboard console. "The light's green," I told her.

We drove on past identical houses with picture

windows. My mother began telling me about a quiz she'd taken that morning in *Mademoiselle*. According to the quiz, she was "emotional," although on the scale of "extrovert" to "introvert," she was an "in-between." If I wanted, she said, she'd let me see her answers, even though they were highly personal.

The Visible Man

That Christmas, our mother gave my brother and me the Visible Man, a scale model of the human body, requiring assembly. When I opened the box, I saw the glassine wrapper into which his organs had been packed, nestled in the clear plastic shell of his body.

"I hope it's not too difficult," my mother said.

Davis began spreading the pieces on the carpet. The mottled blue lungs, the slick nuggest of liver. The grooved cerebellum. The coiled intestines. The glossy pink colon, chambered like a tiny rattlesnake's tail.

I nervously examined the instruction booklet—"written by medical experts," its cover proclaimed. First we would have to assemble his skeleton, which we'd then insert through the opening afforded by his snap-off breastplate. Then we'd have to lay him on his back and gently introduce his vital organs, making sure that each was secured in its proper place, suspended among the others by a kind of concerted pressure, or, otherwise, when he was done and turned upright, he'd come apart. And then, finally, just before mounting him on his display stand, we'd have to paint the plastic casing that was his body with a red and blue roadmap of arteries and veins. I was overwhelmed by the model's enormous complexity. It seemed a terrible responsibility, getting him right.

"Be careful," I told Davis. "You might lose something."

"Don't argue," my mother said. "You have to learn to share him."

As Davis unpacked him, I studied the box-top illustration, which showed how the man would look when fully assembled. It was awful to see him, his arms slightly extended from his sides, as if he were untroubled by showing his own nakedness. Or perhaps—now I was studying his hard, transparent face, molded with tiny, expressionless features—he didn't know how visible he was.

SOME THREADS
THROUGH THE MEDINA

When I left home, I made up this lie: I told everyone my father was French. *Français.*

I said he was the son of a prominent French family that, for obscure reasons, had settled itself in Rabat, Morocco. *Une famille du haut monde. Une famille de fortune aisée.*

I said I was born in Rabat, too, although of course we all fled when the revolution began. *Dans un temp où tout était perdu. Une époque douloureux.*

If people asked about my mother, I said she was a divorced socialite, an American, whom my father had met and married during a sojourn in New York City. He'd found her sitting at the bar in a place called the Three Brothers, wearing her silver fox coat. She had what people called "Spanish eyes," like Gene Tierney in *Leave Her to Heaven. C'est amusant, n'est-ce-pas?*

I have never been to Rabat.

But I have been to Ceuta, although by then my father had been dead for years. After his death, my mother took to her bedroom, where she devoted herself to the lyrical mysteries of the big band music that issued endlessly from her bedside radio. When she drank, even the silence around her said, *Save me.*

As for me: I sat in the dining nook of that suburban house, practicing a foreign language— *je suis . . . tu es . . . il est . . .*

One night I was playing Edith Piaf records in the basement. When I came upstairs, my mother was in the living room in front of the TV, watching an argument on David Susskind's *Open End.*

"Good lord," she said, looking up at me. "Do you have to play those records?"

She reached for her drink. "Just promise me one thing," she said. "Promise me you won't become a homosexual."

In retrospect, of course, I see I had already begun sounding like a homosexual, even though I hated them.

Ten years later, I was in a bar in Torremolinos, where the drunk German beside me kept repeating, *The self is a house you carry with you, the self is a house you carry to the moon . . .*

I thought, *Sure.* That's when I hitched a ride to Algeciras—I wanted to prove I could leave home, even though I'd left my mother's house some years before.

I took the ferry to Ceuta. And the next morning, from Ceuta, I traveled onward in a broken-down Mercedes taxi, the driver smuggling Dior sheets beneath the backseat, to Tetuan and Tangiers.

Would the gentleman care to stop for tea? the driver kept inquiring as we passed through villages deserted to sheep. *Would the gentleman care* . . . We passed three women on the roadside, squatting over an opened suitcase, arguing over a hand mirror. We crossed a bridge where two soldiers with machine guns were guarding a man who was standing with his white caftan lifted to his waist, peeing into the river. When we stopped for gas, children besieged us. *Would the gentleman care* . . . *Would the gentleman care* . . .

By the time we reached Tangiers, I was so fatigued by the assault of newness that I knew I could not fend off the Arab guides who seemed to loiter everywhere—bus stations, markets, hotel lobbies—hoping to catch the eyes of befuddled and frightened tourists, to whom they then bound themselves for days. So the second I stepped from the taxi I allowed myself to be taken up at once by one of them, who, in what seemed a quick moment of cunning, grabbed my suitcase from my hand, vowed his loyalty and his services, and walked promptly up an alleyway dead-ending at a shabby pink stucco palace, the Hôtel du Roi. I followed.

His name was Mohammed. He was eighteen.

He showed me through the medina. "Does one enjoy the taste of these?" he asked gravely, touching a garland of figs. "Does one have an interest in local crafts? In Roman mosaics? Does one admire songbirds?" He showed me how carpet weavers unspooled their coarse bright threads and strung them through eyelets affixed to old planks and stone walls, so that they ran at shoulder height from stall to stall through all the twisting passages of the medina. "One might imagine this red thread traveling to the market's heart," he said, touching its taut circuit along the wall. Then he touched himself lightly on the chest, as if the thread were somehow secured there, knotted to his own heart, although whether he was its origin or its destination I could not tell. "Perhaps if one were lost, one could follow this blue thread," he said. "If one were lost, that is . . ."

Then he turned and was suddenly standing by a gaudy stall, sorting through racks and racks of tape cassettes. He motioned for me to join him. "Do you like *Abbey Road*," he asked, "or this one called *Mellow Yellow*?" He said that if he were simply choosing for himself, he imagined he might particularly enjoy four or five cassettes featuring the melodies of Oum Kalthoum of Egypt.

So that's the pitch, I thought. Perhaps, if he had more time to give, he might particularly enjoy new shoes as well. When I left, I assured him I had my bearings.

But the next morning when I emerged from the hotel, I found him sitting at the curb as though he'd been waiting since daybreak. Whether his patience derived from his promised loyalty or whether he was leery that I was trying to ditch him, I did not know. "Today we will tour Tangiers," he said. "Today we will start with the ramparts."

For hours as we walked, first ascending steep stone steps, then coming down through dark passageways that opened onto crowded, sunstruck boulevards, he kept telling me how much he hoped to visit New York City and how much he liked the Motown sound, especially the songs by James Brown. Once, when I stopped to price some postcards, I thought I glimpsed him crossing the busy plaza, his bright blue T-shirt fluttering like a flag, and when I looked up to check, I saw he'd joined some Arab boys who were standing in a doorway, sharing a cigarette and laughing. "Those were my brothers," he later explained, although I knew it wasn't so, since he'd already told me his family lived far south, below Tafraoute.

He proposed that we eat lunch. While we finished a chicken stewed in a brine of olives, he showed me the half-dozen letters he'd received from German and American tourists he had guided around Tangiers. They were short letters, written on aerograms and onionskin paper, and in a simple and hesitant language that hinted at the stilted syntax they had used with him, their authors assured him of the quality of his company, telling him how in their fond hearts it was he, Mohammed, dearest Mohammed, who stood for the soul of Morocco. Sometimes there were snapshots enclosed—a heavy German blonde in a crocheted pink bikini, posed by an emptied pool;

an angular, pock-marked man standing on a sun-bleached concrete driveway, holding a chihuahua.

"I am hoping," Mohammed said, carefully refolding a sheet of fragile blue paper, "that one day you shall write me such a letter."

The waiter cleared our dishes. I asked for a bottle of water.

In this way, we went on for hours. We looked at a mosque encircled by an iron fence topped with barbed wire. We sat on a bench in an unkempt garden. "I could tell you the names of flowers in Arabic," he said.

Then, when it was dark, he steered me back through the narrow streets of the medina toward the Hôtel du Roi, where, for a moment, there was an awkward silence at the door. *And now what?* I thought. *Would the gentleman care . . . ?* Seen from a distance—by the veiled woman I saw glancing at us from an upstairs window, perhaps—we must have looked like strangers pausing to give the time or to buy hashish, or like paramours shyly parting.

"Are you really so tired?" Mohammed asked, standing half within the building's shadow, desultorily picking at the pink stucco wall until paint chips fell to his sandals. Then he touched me lightly on the elbow, as though he meant to take my arm, the way Moroccan men did when they walked with one another, and his touch so exhilarated me—*He is beautiful*, I thought, *and nothing like me*—that I instantly imagined its possible intention as some ludicrous and sad contrivance of my own. Certainly he was simply attempting to negotiate whether or not I'd value his presence at the hotel door the next morning. But why should he? Certainly his presence was a fait accompli, for if there was one thing people said of all these guides, it was that they simply couldn't be shaken.

In this way, the debate I conducted within myself wore down my own desire. "Good night," I said. "I'm very tired. Very tired." Truly, I could not figure how to tell him just how tired I was.

That is, I could not figure how to tell him that I wanted him to come to my room. My room was preposterously simple, if not in its execution, then in its mentality. On the right was a plasticized orange valet chair, presumably for *monsieur*. On the left was a bidet concealed behind a tattered green curtain, presumably for *madame*. In the middle was a sagging bed, presumably for pleasure. *Une chambre très bon confort. Un hôtel très agréable.* In retrospect, of course, I see Mohammed would have fucked me, if that was what I really wanted, or, perhaps, he might even have allowed himself to be fucked, after modestly preparing himself in the bidet behind the tattered curtain. In retrospect I see there was a way of telling him what I wanted, and doing so quite simply—words, for instance, or money, preferably in dollars or Deutsche marks, although, if necessary, pesetas might also have been accepted.

In retrospect I even see that Mohammed himself had wanted this—I don't mean just the

104

money—for on my fifth day in Tangiers, we argued and he stormed off like an angry lover, abandoning me in the medina.

That morning, we had gone to a beach outside the city. For two days, we had been rehearsing the details of this excursion. For two days, I had been imagining us as we would be—lying side by side in the sun. I had imagined how the heat would calm us and how the cold water would startle us to life.

But the public bus was crowded, and the ride went on forever, through miles of industrial sites. When at last the beach was visible along one side of the highway, it looked mean and narrow, strung with power lines. Where the road ran out, the bus stopped, near a Quonset hut where an old man was selling fireworks and oranges.

At first we tried to lie on the small blanket he'd brought along. But the wind drove us to take shelter by a concrete wall beside a culvert. In the distance I could see a small girl dragging a rope through a pool of stagnant water. Nearby, a boy was slashing old tires with a knife.

"This is a terrible place," Mohammed said. "You can't like it here. It is terrible."

I wondered if he had ever really been here before. Back in Tangiers, he'd claimed to love the beach. He'd claimed to love it more than anywhere. He had said he'd spent whole days swimming in the ocean and that he'd spent evenings dancing at discothèques where he had met amusing people.

But now he looked simply worn and tired. He sat beside me, brushing sand from his bare ankles, then smoothing the legs of his trousers. He had brought neither a swimsuit nor a change of clothes.

He stood up. "I will get us something to eat," he said.

He crossed a small stretch of sand and climbed onto the shoulder of the road. He started down the blacktop toward the Quonset hut. After a while, he returned, carrying a bag of oranges.

He held the bag aloft. "I am bringing us these suns!" he shouted. "I am bringing us a whole bag of them! More suns than we can use!" As he came down the beach toward me, he did a small dance, jumping from one foot to the other and then hoisting the bag of oranges into the air. When he stopped, he rotated the bag around his head, as if the oranges were orbiting there.

"It's cold," I said.

He sat down against the concrete wall and pressed an orange to his mouth. "You should eat something," he said, pushing the bag toward me.

But I said nothing. I watched him as he devoured one orange and then another.

Then he gathered the rinds into a pile. When he looked up, he suggested we return to the city. "I know where you can get some very nice shoes," he said, resuming what I took to be his old theme. "I know a man who sells nice shoes. All very nice. All handmade. Completely leather." Then he pointed to his plastic sandals. "Not like these," he said. "These are terrible."

He began to enumerate the many places he knew where one could buy an inlaid box or a discount watch or a dozen calfskin wallets. "Have you seen the ceramics of Fez?" he asked. And soon we were passing through the lower gates of the medina, following the weaver's blue thread, for I had allowed that I might be interested in something woven, if it was small enough to take along—like a prayer rug, perhaps. We passed cages of pigeons beating their wings. We passed an open hearth where a Berber was tempering knives. The whole way, Mohammed kept saying, "I know you will like this merchant. I know you will admire the things he arranges to sell."

When he saw Mohammed, the merchant rose from his stool to greet us. *"Salaamu'aleikum,"* he said, shaking my hand. Then he busied himself, unbinding a dozen small carpets and arranging them around his stall. *"Le monsieur, qu'est-qui'il préfére?"* he asked Mohammed. *"Le tapis rouge? Le gris? Le bleu?"*

When at last I chose a rug, Mohammed said he would haggle in Arabic on my behalf. He carried the rug into the sunlight to assess its imperfections. He slowly examined each knot of its fringe.

The merchant followed him into the light. *"Que vous êtes fou!"* the merchant shouted, quite instantly irritated. *"Imshee!* Go away!"

Then Mohammed turned the rug over to count its threads.

"Na'am!" said the merchant. And Mohammed said, *"Lah!"* They haggled for half an hour. They haggled so long that I began to imagine the beach had never been anything more than a detour that was calculated to carry me down the narrowing passages that led finally to the blind alley where I now stood. They haggled so long that I wanted to go.

Then they settled on a price.

But I thought I saw Mohammed and the merchant smile, as if in concert.

Mohammed turned toward me. "A good value?"

I hesitated. *"Well . . ."*

And in that instant Mohammed saw that I feared he was cheating me.

At first he looked embarrassed, as if he held himself responsible for having invented some affection he had imagined to be mutual. Then he looked at me directly, as if seeking some confirmation—or, more precisely, some denial—of the reality my hesitation had created.

But I looked away. After all, there was certainly no reason for him to be upset. After all, my caution was hardly personal.

He was furious.

He picked up the bag of oranges he had bought and shoved his way past me into the street. Then he turned and threw the oranges to the ground and the bag split and the fruit ruptured, its bright juice puddling on the cobblestones. He shouted that I should keep them, they were his gift, *un souvenir trés symbolique*. Surely I could appreciate *that*, even if there was little else about him I seemed to understand. *"Évidemment, monsieur,"* he said, *"vous ne savez rien de Maroc. Ni des hommes. Ni de moi."*

My god, I thought as he walked away, *he's practically flouncing*.

Then I saw that the merchants were watching me, and I imagined they found me at fault, as if I'd made some untoward suggestion that Mohammed had naturally rebuffed in the clearest and most necessary manner, and to show how unperturbed I was—it was nothing, *nothing*, like they imagined—I turned toward one of them, the one who seemed the least successful, the most wretched, the most needy, and I said, "I *assume* your rugs are handmade. I assume they are *originals*."

I made my way back to the Hôtel du Roi—to the lobby with its dirty banquettes and its caged reception desk, where the concierge presided over the room keys as though they were racks of pawn-shop watches. I hated the concierge: each night when I came in, leaving Mohammed at the curb, I hated finding him in his steel cage, regarding me steadily as he sipped his mint tea; I hated asking him for my room key, the number of which he must surely by then have memorized; I hated the way he dropped the key onto the counter, as if it were something he were selling to me, an undiscerning customer who had chosen an utterly unattractive item of the very poorest quality; and I hated the way, as he pushed it forward, he smiled unctuously, as though to tell me my bad choice would surely cost me, but if that was what I wanted, then, *alors,* what could he do but oblige me? *Caveat emptor.* That is, each night after I left Mohammed at the curb, I imagined the concierge had witnessed my desire and that he'd disapproved of it, and of me, and of all my kind—my kind! what kind was that?—although, in retrospect, I see that if he was angry it was probably because I'd denied him the small bribe it would have taken to get Mohammed past his desk.

"Peut-être monsieur désire autres choses?" Perhaps monsieur desires a newspaper? A nightcap? Anything at all?

"Non," I said, *"monsieur ne désire rien."* Nothing, that is, except to get past you, past you and into that elevator that will lift me upward, shaking on its loose cables as it rises.

I went to my room and lay down. It was then that I thought to go to Rabat. After all, I thought, it might be amusing to visit Rabat, since I'd talked so much about it once upon a time; and, of course, Rabat had a reputation quite different from that of Tangiers. In the scheme of Morocco, in fact, Rabat was often considered somewhat quiet and even disappointing, although such opinions tended toward the highly touristic, formed by those least well equipped to get the feel of a place. But when it came right down to it, Tangiers was really a bit more like Tijuana than anywhere. One could hardly judge a whole country by its borders.

This was a good plan. But first I would get a good sleep—a very good sleep—and when I got up, I would probably find Mohammed sitting at the curb outside the hotel, as I always did, and I would explain that I was headed to Rabat, and, if he liked and had the time, I would be pleased if he'd be my guest for a glass of tea before I headed for the station. While we had the tea, I'd find an inoffensive way to settle up, since, after all, he had shown me around the entire city and had done so quite intelligently. Not that it was rare, the thing about the money. Indeed, it was the custom— or so I'd heard—to present the money at the parting, so that it seemed like more of what it was, a deeply felt and well-intentioned gift, and not a series of demeaning tips awarded for specific services performed.

But of course when I came down the next morning, there was no Mohammed.

There was only the concierge—and beside him, also locked within the metal cage, was an Arab child, a boy. The boy was crying. The concierge was punishing him. I could not make out the offense. What carries us to places that express us better than we might express ourselves, so that were someone to ask, "What's the matter?" we might point mutely—"This . . ."?

The concierge looked up at me. "There's no message from your friend," he said, "if that's what you're waiting for."

The concierge unlocked the cage and pushed the boy, still crying, through the door. "Go on," he said. "Get out of here."

The boy hurried into the street. Then the concierge busied himself, copying sums from one black ledger into another. I simply stood there. I was trying to make up my mind. There was a hydrofoil leaving for the Spanish coast at eleven a.m.

The concierge put down his pencil. "Is there something else?" he asked, annoyed. "Look, if it's about the kid, he'll come back. He always does. He's my son."

So, he was his son.

And then I was crossing the Spanish frontier at Tarifa, its beach lined with army tanks. And then I was in Torremolinos, and from Torremolinos I hitched a ride with a drunk countess—"*Le roi est mort!*" she kept shouting from her Fiat's open window—to Alicante, where she lived, and from Alicante I took a bus to Barcelona, and from Barcelona I boarded a train for the border at Port Bou. And at midnight in Port Bou, as I waited on the concrete quay for the Paris Express, a blonde woman kept staring at me as if I were familiar, until at last she asked, "*Sind Sie auch Deutsch?*"

"No, I'm not German," I said. "I'm something

else." But I was thinking, *There's really quite a word for what I am.*

And then I was drunk, and I was in Paris, and I was at the Cinema Marotte, on Rue Vivienne, sitting beside a Filipino who rubbed my crotch as he stared in silence at a movie of two men fucking, one with his legs raised, slavish and demanding, and the other, mounting him, brutal and apologetic. The two men were muscled like Americans. *"C'est amusant, n'est-ce-pas?"* the Filipino whispered; he smelled faintly of the restaurant he must have worked in. Then he withdrew a handkerchief, which he fluttered briefly in the dark before dropping it to my lap, where he held it—*"Vite, ça viens"*—as I came. Onscreen the actors exchanged roles, and the one who'd been on the bottom became wildly angry, unbelievably so, like a furious cartoon character, or maybe the movie itself changed, I don't remember—*séances continuelles*.

And then I was alone again, and drunker still, and standing on the pavement, staring into a shop window filled with dusty stuffed iguanas and dying cacti, and in the rear of the shop, I could see five small lighted clocks that told time in major cities around the world, and beneath them, a banner: *Agence des voyages. Traversez par tôut l'universe*. In New York, it was late; in Paris, later still.

I hailed a taxi.

And then I realized I could go anywhere, turn right, turn left, drive dead on for a million miles, *traversez par tôut l'univers*, and I threw my cigarette

113

to the gutter, for at that moment I realized I could give up anything, even smoking—I had no more dependencies.

A taxi stopped and I climbed in. The driver was a corpulent middle-aged woman with her German shepherd sitting on the front seat beside her.

"Hôtel Saint-Séverin," I said, although this wasn't really what I wanted. I simply didn't know how to direct her to drive on forever. Where was a phrase book, an emergency lexicon? *Farther, farther, just get me out of here . . .*

I must have scared her with my drunkenness, for as she drove she watched me in her rearview mirror. She studied me so long and so intently, in fact, I began talking. I talked so much I couldn't stop. "I have always wanted to be in Paris," I told her. "It is all I have ever wanted. My whole life, since I was a teenager speaking French—well, for most of my life, then. Since hearing Edith Piaf."

When I said "Piaf," the driver eyed me in the mirror yet more narrowly. She speeded up.

"When I was a child," I rattled on, "I listened to Piaf. I listened to Piaf in the basement rec room. 'Mon Dieu,' 'La Vie en Rose,' 'Je Ne Regrette Rien.' I unscrewed the shade from the floor lamp and stood in front of it as if it were my spotlight. Then I lip-synched to her records—*Ladies and gentlemen, I give you Edith Piaf! Tonight, the Little Sparrow!* I have always wanted to be in Paris. It is all I ever wanted. In *Paris*. All that time."

We were crossing Pont Neuf when the driver

slammed on her brakes. Her German shepherd was pitched against the dashboard, and suddenly we were stopped in the middle of the bridge.

The driver turned to face me. *"Mais monsieur,"* she said, *"vous êtes à Paris. Voilà! Notre Dame!"* And indeed, when I looked to my left, there it was, Notre Dame.

I felt sober.

How long had I been traveling? And how far away? And from what fixed point outside myself? There had been the club in Berlin where I'd watched the American soldier dancing with himself in a mirror, and the pensione in Budapest where I'd seen the old man sitting at his vanity, applying pancake makeup to his face. "Shall you come in?" he'd asked, when he looked up and found me standing at his doorway. There had been the field at night along the river in Trier, and the abandoned Luna Park near Vicenza, and the public washroom of the train station in Zurich.

But I had gone nowhere. Nowhere at all. I was sitting in a taxi stopped on a bridge, watching the driver pet her German shepherd. For a moment, I wondered if the Tuileries Gardens were nearby. I had heard what men did there at night, by the back gate that led to the Orangerie.

Then the drunk feeling started again, the feeling that would last for years.

I wanted to say something to the driver. I thought she might understand. "My father always said he hoped that I'd see Notre Dame," I began.

But she was looking out her window. *All right,* I thought. *Just look away then—I suppose you think you're the soul of France . . .*

"We lived in Morocco," I continued. "In the days before the independence, before the Moroccans made themselves into such a mob of Abduls and Mohammeds." When I leaned forward to tell her this, I could see myself in the rearview mirror. I could see a part of my face and mouth moving as I spoke.

FUGITIVE LIGHT, OLD PHOTOS

At the morgue, the attendant showed us two Polaroids.

In one, my brother Davis was prone. In the other, he'd been turned faceup on a steel examining table. *Who combed his hair so neatly?* I wondered. *Who gave him that bright blue T-shirt?* But in the flashbulb's glare, his face looked mottled, the way a sleeper's face is sometimes marked by the imprint of his blanket so that he seems to be bearing a harsh dream's souvenir.

"That's not my son," my mother said, putting the Polaroids down on the counter. She said she would have to see the body.

But the attendant returned to his desk—green metal, like government-issue. He read from his clipboard: We couldn't see the body unless we had prior written permission, he said, since actual viewing was no longer the standard procedure. Then he resumed his work, watching *Soul Train* on a miniature TV.

I know I should have argued with him, as my mother wanted. I know I should have insisted.

But I wanted to see nothing further: not the tiled

corridors, nor the refrigerated units, those rows of identical steel doors. After all, wasn't it enough to have cleared Davis's garbage-strewn apartment, to have disposed of the urine-soaked mattress on which he died, dragging it down three flights of stairs to his building's alleyway Dumpster? And afterward, when the police came to search his apartment for evidence, wasn't it enough to have hidden his used syringes at the bottom of a grocery bag, beneath old newspapers, like ordinary garbage? Davis was thirty-five. He had died of a drug overdose.

I signed the papers.

All the way home, I tried to reassure my mother. I told her, "That was really Davis whose photo we saw."

We had his body cremated. There is no body anymore.

Here is Davis at six, shrill with laughter, embracing our father's cocker spaniel, who is lying, feet up, on the lawn. Here is Davis at eight, conspicuous in the back row of his fourth-grade photo, burdened by the brown patch the doctor has affixed to his eyeglasses. And here is Davis at twelve, standing at the swim club, awkwardly shielding his pubescent body with a towel.

"You don't know this," my mother tells me. "But Davis was a blue baby. When he was born, there were critical seconds when he didn't get air."

We are sitting at her dining room table, beneath

118

a bright ceiling light, in the small retirement house where she lives with her third husband, who sequesters himself in the den each night, watching TV alone. My mother and I are sorting through old black-and-white photos with scalloped borders, making a scrapbook of Davis's life. "Look," she says, handing me a photo of Davis as a baby, toddling across a lawn of cut grass, holding an Easter basket.

"That's why he cried too much," she adds. "The doctor came to my room after the delivery. He told me that because Davis was a blue baby, he could have serious trouble later on."

What does she want me to tell her? That Davis could not be comforted because something terrible had happened to him in the abrupt moment between being taken from her body and being delivered, crying, into her arms?

I could just as well remind her how Davis had laughed with pleasure whenever our father called him Davy Crockett.

He was thin and graceless. His teachers labeled him a slow learner.

When I was angry at him, she made me recite, "Let me be a little meeker / With the brother who is weaker."

But I know what she wants. She is seventy-one. She tells me that I am her best friend, now that most of her friends have died.

She wants me to say, "He was a blue baby. A long time ago, there were critical seconds when he didn't get air." She wants me to caption these flimsy Kodaks—these proofs of happy impetuosities, of sudden Saturday outings, of picnics and festive hats fashioned from aluminum foil—so she can mount them onto the huge black pages of the scrapbook she has bought.

Instead, I hand her the photo of Davis toddling across the lawn.

None of this—not even this snapshot, with its streaks of light—is the past I now recall. I see how Davis stares dazedly at the camera, as if drowsy and fretful in the noonday heat. And suddenly I want to draw him close, to offer him my protection.

"Look," I tell her. "By 'trouble,' I don't think the doctor meant that Davis was going to die of a heroin overdose."

She is silent, as if to tell me that I have hurt her. We have not discussed the autopsy report she has received: "Needle punctures involving right forearm . . . ," "Kidneys, 300 gms., no gross focal lesions, sections not remarkable . . . ," "Lividity . . ." Then she busies herself. "That isn't what I meant," she says. "I was just trying to explain a theory."

She holds a photograph beneath the table lamp and examines it. Then she chooses another. "I remember every detail," she says.

Don't, I tell myself. After all, it is only a snapshot of Davis in cutoff jeans, lying on our porch glider. It's only a snapshot of Davis washing our old two-tone Chevy.

But suddenly, in a long drop, before I can stop myself, I am falling, weightless and unconstrained, through all the unphotographed moments of her rages and her terrors, toward memories that rise beneath me like hard earth. She comes to our room at night, searching the house for cigarettes, whispering accusations—*Why can't you ever . . . , I shouldn't have hoped . . . , If you would only . . .* By morning she is sprawled in her beige slip on the basement daybed, her silver bracelets—her "lucky bangles," as she calls them—discarded in a crystal ashtray. She murmurs in her sleep—*Don't let . . . , I never hated . . . , Not harmed . . .*

Sometimes, after school, we find her waiting in her Impala convertible at the edge of the parking lot, her face obscured by the sun visor's deliberate black slash. When we open the car door and get in, sliding across the wide vinyl seat, we find her strangely girlish and tearfully apologetic. Other times, when she is not there, we walk home slowly, past a power station and across a divided highway, and then on through acres of identical subdivisions, afraid to find that she's angry at us again when we get home.

Listen, do you really want a theory so badly? Then here is my theory: You were supposed to be the mother, but you let your child die.

And again I am returned to those long, fatherless nights of our adolescence, when Davis and I sat on the back porch, beside a black iron railing, still waiting for the appearance of late-blooming constellations, as if our father's impassive face might appear to us among them.

Our mother sat in her bedroom, listening to a radio call-in show. "Dear hearts," the deejay whispered. "It's late. I know you're lonely."

Go to her, Davis and I would argue.

For a moment, when I look up, I am not sure who she is—this woman who sits beside me, sorting old photos; this woman who has hung a stained-glass Serenity Prayer in her kitchen window. *She is an old woman*, I tell myself. *She lives in an old woman's house*. There are her floe blue plates, displayed on shelves along the wall. There are her tiered end tables, neatly arranged with bric-a-brac. There are her cut-glass dishes, filled with sugarless candies. There is scarcely anything of her husband's to be seen.

"I have to go," I tell her. Soon she will need to check her blood sugar.

I know she is disappointed. I know these photographs have awakened in her a story she has no one else to tell. But tonight, I cannot hear how as an infant Davis cried when anyone approached him. How he feared crowds so badly, she could not take him on the streetcar.

Tonight, I want no stories. Tonight, I want only the singular, precise moments of these snapshots—these snapshots reversed from negatives, these sensitive emulsions dependent on even the briefest, most fugitive light. Tonight, I want only the singular, precise moments of everything that remains unfixed, unsorted, not yet pasted to its final page.

"All right," my mother says. "We can finish our scrapbook later." She starts to gather loose photographs from the table. "You haven't told me why you think he died," she says.

"Drugs," I tell her. "He died of a drug overdose."

"I know," she says. "But that isn't what I'm asking."

I tell her I will straighten the table. I cap the bottle of white ink we have used for writing captions; I wipe it with a paper towel. Then I set it inside an old shoe box, alongside the loose photos she has gathered. She carries the shoe box to her bedroom, to store in what she calls her "memory drawer."

When she comes back, she is carrying a large manila envelope. She says she has filled it with photos she thinks I'll want to have.

Then she sees me to the door.

For a moment, we pause beneath the yellow porch light. From there, the boxwoods bordering the garage seem almost blue, dense with luminescence. "Good night," she says.

"Good night," I say. I walk to the car. But when I turn to wave good-bye, I see she has already closed the front door.

I get in the car. I switch on the dome light. I open the manila envelope.

It is not filled with photos of Davis, as I expected.

Instead, it is filled with old photos I studied as a child for hours, drifting through them—long rainy Saturdays, sitting on the screened-in porch; whole summer afternoons, lying on the cool tiles of the basement floor—until I grew so mesmerized, I could scarcely recall my own name. Here is my mother at six, nervously stroking a spotted pony, her bangs cut short across her forehead. And here she is at fifteen, standing on the broad lawn of her parents' summer house, smiling at the suitor who has just filled her arms with cut hydrangeas, in order to take her picture just this way. And here she is in the photo I loved best, taken during her first marriage, when she was barely twenty. The photo is torn. But within it she calmly regards herself in her dresser mirror, so that one sees her as she sees herself, reflected, a stargazer lily pinned to her dark hair. On its back she has written, "I looked like Merle Oberon."

But where is the photo of the night Davis was first arrested? I was there.

Two policemen had brought him back to the house. They said they'd caught him in a Safeway parking lot selling marijuana to minors. He was eighteen.

From where I stood on the living room threshold, everyone seemed so still, I thought they would turn into a photo. *Click*, I thought. *Click*.

Then my mother leaned forward. "Get out of my sight," she told Davis.

What could I have said to him then? Or what

could I have said the second time he was arrested, in a police roundup in a park where men went at night for sex? What could I have said the night he phoned from jail to tell me that his headaches had grown so fierce, he thought he would pluck out his eyes?

Once, she was beautiful.

Once, a man gave her cut flowers.

We are all of us blue babies. At critical seconds, we all lack necessary air.

My mother shuts off the porch light. The lawn falls into darkness.

I put the key in the ignition and start the car.

But when I look up, I see my mother framed in her front bay window, walking back through her living room, carrying the shoe box of old photos. She has changed into her housecoat. For a moment she disappears into the darkened doorway of the kitchen. Then she returns with a glass of water and seats herself at the dining room table.

She turns on the lamp. She leans forward. She opens the shoe box. She chooses a photo and lifts it into the sharp white light.

No, I want to warn her. *What you are doing is too difficult. Too difficult and wrong.*

But she works on. She studies the photo closely, as if she imagines the steady effort of her attention will force it to yield whatever mystery it might hold. She examines it beneath a magnifying glass. What year is it for her, as she sits at her dining room table? What does she see now, outside that photo's glossy white border?

Watching her, I imagine her standing on our front lawn in a flowered sundress, holding a box camera, as years ago she must have done. She wants to take a picture of her son.

Her sundress flutters in the spring wind. With one hand she balances the box camera. Then she extends her free hand toward Davis, who sits before her on the lawn.

"Davis," she coaxes. "Davis, come."

And when he stands and at last takes a toddling step toward her, she presses the shutter, and, through the view-finder, she sees her own life walking precariously toward her, with his arms outstretched.

Don't die, I whisper.

But she can't hear me. She pastes the photograph onto the black page. She reaches into the shoe box. She chooses another. When she finishes the page, she turns it slowly; slowly, as if turning the page were the last thing she wanted to do.

EDUARDO'S HAIR

A year later I found myself at a crowded party in a pine-paneled beach cottage, lying on a narrow bed beside a man named Paul—a friend of a friend, a model up from New York City for the weekend—who was pressing his ear to the fluted pink edge of a conch shell so he could hear the ocean sound of his own head. *Oh*, I kept thinking as I watched him, *he has Eduardo's hair*. I didn't know if I wanted to tell him this, since he wouldn't have known that Eduardo was the man I had loved all the difficult years before. In truth, I didn't know if those years were really over, and I didn't know if I would ever want to say to anyone again, "You sure have beautiful hair."

I first met Eduardo in a piano bar when I was thirty-three and he was thirty-four. I stood in a corner watching him while he talked and drank with some Latin guys I used to know. *I would love to touch his hair*, I thought—thick and black, with a faint trace of silver at each temple, barely noticeable, like a premonition.

That was what desire was like in those days, in

127

case no one remembers—sudden and absolute, so that the sharp blue electric arc of wanting leapt quickly from the pole of impulse to the opposite pole of action. The next night we met for dinner in a rooftop restaurant that has long since gone out of business. When he leaned over the table toward me, I touched his hair.

Over the next seven years, I often had the opportunity to run a hand through his hair. At night sometimes, when making love, or afterward, shampooing each other in the shower. Or in the morning, when we sat at our breakfast table, Eduardo hurriedly eating his cereal before work. I'd come up from behind him and touch him on the head, and then, because he was an attorney who appeared often in courtrooms, I'd say, "Before you leave, don't forget to comb your hair."

In the months after his diagnosis, I suppose I was thinking mostly of the time that would come when he would be sick and I would be the one to wash and cut his hair. For a long time, I was afraid of everything that was evidence of the physical life we shared: our razors lying side by side on the porcelain sink; toothbrushes nestling in a water glass smeared with handprints; black hair strung in greasy knots that I sometimes pulled up while snaking the drain of the tub. At night when I lay beside him, I was afraid of the things his body was emitting or sloughing off—like his cum puddling on his belly after he jacked off, or like the night sweats that soaked the sheets in which we slept. My self-diagnosis, looking back? A fear of nail trimmings; a fear of mitosis; a fear of cells dividing and failing.

What could I have said to him? Our language had always been touch—a late-night language with its own grammar of pleasure and consolation, its inflections of sorrow. We had never located a bright corridor of words that would allow us to move with ease toward one another.

I remember driving him home one night from signing the power of attorney and the document that would one day give me the right to decide when Eduardo would die.

"Well," said Eduardo, after miles and miles. "Well. There."

"Yes," I said. "That's right. There."

In the last months of his life, I was afraid of the time when he would be neither here nor there. By then his body had sloughed off almost everything, including the things he most needed: he weighed less than one hundred pounds, and his skin bruised and bled each time the visiting nurse held his arms to hoist him from his bed onto the toilet. By then his meals were delivered by an agency of caregivers—I just had to put the food on a plate and carry it up the stairs. Most nights he raged at the health aides who came to flush his heplock and to bathe him with damp towels scented with cologne. The aides were women from far away—from Nigeria, for instance, and Haiti—and sometimes when I was lonely I sat with them in the TV room, watching them while they addressed greeting cards to their families back home or while they fiddled with their elaborately plaited and coiled hair.

An ambulance took him to the hospital. I know what people saw that scared them when they looked into his room while passing down the corridor on the way to the coffee machine— his face like a mask stretched taut on a skull, matchstick arms and legs affixed to a torso swollen with fluids, jaundiced skin almost the color of mahogany. When he was awake, we watched TV or flipped through magazines. But when he slept, I was desperate to study his body. "Where are you taking us?" I wanted to ask it—or someone.

The last day, he had three seizures, one after the other, and when they were finished, it seemed he had at last sloughed off everything—except for his rages and their subsequent exhaustions. "Don't touch me, you cocksucker!" he yelled at the orderly who was tying him to the bed.

He looked at me as I stood there. "What do you think you're doing?" he said. "What the fuck do you think you're doing now?"

I didn't know what to tell him, although I knew it was wrong to restrain him when he was leaving his life behind. I said I was keeping an eye on him, as I had always done. But he didn't believe it. He shook his head: *No, no.*

"Calm down," I said.

I put my hand on his forehead. "Eduardo, please calm down," I said. "I've come to comb your hair."

MY BROTHER IN THE BASEMENT

He was dark; I was fair.

He was slender and shy; I was stocky and talkative.

As children our mother dressed us as twins. Matching woolen peacoats and Buster Brown lace-ups, khaki shorts and striped T-shirts, pajamas imprinted with pictures of cowboys and Indians, Davy Crockett coonskin caps. For Easter, matching sailor suits with starched white middy blouses.

Even so, the neighbors often strained to see the resemblance between us. "You're brothers?" they asked. "You're really brothers? Which one of you is older?"

People imagined I was, because I was larger. But in fact he was older, by fifteen months. The bassinet into which I was placed was still warm from his having so recently lain there.

Was it paradise, living like that, with someone made of the same flesh and blood as I? When Davis and I were little, we lay awake at night in our bunk beds, devising a language only the two of us could understand. "Peanut butter" meant

"I'm sorry." "Bongo bongo" meant "Go to sleep." "Applesauce" meant "Laugh!"

Sometimes when I crawled into his upper bunk to lie beside him, my shoulder touching his, I believed we were living together in just one body.

Not that we were identical. Not that we were even twins. Abel was a keeper of sheep; Cain, a tiller of soil.

Was that our story, except with the roles reversed? I was younger, like Abel. But I lived. And it wasn't as if I killed my brother, not really, even if it sometimes felt as though I did.

Of course, it could just as well have been I who died, had it not been for what he once referred to—it was an accusation, he was angry—as my "instinct for survival." That was what my mother and I had in common, he said—no ideals or principles; nothing, nothing, except our instincts to survive.

He meant: Why have I come out to our mother while you continue avoiding to do so? Why am I the one who must bear her displeasure? Why have you left me here standing alone?

"It must be great," people used to say to me, "being gay and having a gay brother. You two must feel a special closeness. Like having a twin."

Of course, if the people who said these things were the men Davis and I met the nights we went cruising together in gay bars, they meant something rather different by their words. They meant: Do you guys ever have sex with each other? Have you *done* it? Would you like to do a three-way?

"No, we don't have sex with each other," I said. "No, we're not looking for a three-way."

I was like that in those days, even in the leather bars Davis liked to frequent. A little prim. A little earnest.

But Davis liked to joke with the men who approached us: "Yeah, sure, why not?" he said. "Maybe if you buy us enough drinks. Maybe if you give us enough money."

"Davis," I whispered when the men weren't looking. "Don't talk that way. They might believe you."

It's 1957, or maybe it's 1958, certainly no later than that, and Davis and I are walking home from Carroll Knolls Elementary—through a small complex of garden apartments, past the First United Methodist Church—discussing what we will do if our parents are ever killed suddenly together in a car crash, or a plane wreck, or a bomb attack, like at Pearl Harbor. We'll build ourselves a cabin in the woods, we decide, where no one will ever find us. We'll light our cabin with candles and support ourselves with newspaper routes—the *Montgomery County Sentinel*, the *Catholic Standard*, the *Washington Star*.

Was that the first time we began dreaming of a house where we would one day live together? I

134

thought I would have him as my family forever, no matter what. Wherever he was, I thought, would be my home.

On Saturday mornings, for instance, when the other boys in our neighborhood were practicing softball, Davis and I were riding our bicycles to new subdivisions, touring the model homes for hours, navigating the narrow trails of plastic runners the real estate agents lay down to protect the new wall-to-wall carpeting, through living rooms and rumpus rooms and dining nooks and master suites with walk-in closets, through split-levels and Cape Cods and two-story colonials and ranch houses with finished basements and picture windows.

We liked houses with laundry chutes and intercom systems and carports.

We liked floor plans, which we studied in photo-illustrated magazines we swiped from drugstores—*101 Dream Houses, 101 A-Frames, 101 Modular Homes You Can Build on a Budget.*

On Sundays, after Mass, we liked to visit the mobile home lots off the more populous highways, the ones strung with out-of-season Christmas lights and bright tricornered flags, where the salesmen were more likely to let us wander unescorted through the latest 10'x 50' models: the Skyline Diamond, with its frost-free jalousie windows; the Saratoga, with its tip-out room and simulated fireplace with artificial logs; the Space Master, with its sky roof and circular kitchen. The

Vagabond. The Ventura. The New Moon. The Crestline Viceroy. The Magnolia. The Starflite.

"Look at this; it's so beautiful," I said to Davis as I demonstrated the ease of the Starflite's pocket doors, how they slid effortlessly back and forth on their plastic tracks.

"We'll all live like this one day in the future," he told me.

Here is a fact: My brother was arrested three times. Twice for the possession and distribution of controlled substances, including marijuana, amphetamines, psilocybin, and Quaaludes. And once again—the middle arrest, when he was twenty-six—for sodomy, public indecency, and lewd and lascivious acts. Meaning: He was caught in a sudden police roundup in the public toilets of a park where men went at night to have sex.

"Go fuck yourself," he told the cop who put him in handcuffs.

But later, in lockup, when the desk officer told him it was time for his one phone call, he thought he might just as well kill himself as call our mother. At least that's what he told me later.

(That's what it was in the old days, in case anyone who has tuned in to this late-night broadcast has happened to forget: sudden arrest; your name in the papers the next morning; then, maybe, a quiet suicide. One, two, three, just like

136

a game of hopscotch, except you had to play bare-foot, jumping on broken glass.)

As for me: I was 1,200 miles away, in graduate school, the time he was arrested for sex. My mother told me about it in a phone call.

"Maybe I shouldn't post his bail this time," she said. "Maybe he keeps getting in trouble because he knows I'll come to his rescue. Maybe I should just let him sit there."

"Mom," I said, "you have to bail him out. Just go and do it. Do it now."

Otherwise, I stayed as far away as I could. By then, Davis and our mother had begun their endless arguments with each other. Watching them argue was like looking back at a burning house I'd just fled. Even though I was running hard in the opposite direction, I could hear the windows shattering from the heat and the roof beams collapsing onto the walls.

I mean: I was afraid. I hid my life from her. My homo life, that is, which consisted then mostly of daydreams in which men held me close and assured me it was all right if I was afraid.

As for my other life, I didn't mind sharing that: diplomas, fellowships, job offers, vacation plans. "Mom, guess what!" I told her on the phone. "The professors voted me teaching assistant of the year!" Or: "I was in New York City, Mom, and I went to Rockefeller Plaza to watch the ice skaters, just like you did growing up."

That is, I gave her what I had always given her:

I was the good son. I was the mirror in which she saw her own life made more meaningful and lustrous.

How does that story go? *And in process of time it came to pass, that Cain brought of the fruit of the ground an offering unto the Lord. And Abel, he also brought of the firstlings of his flock and the fat thereof. And the Lord had respect unto his Abel and his offering. But unto Cain he had no respect. And Cain was very wroth, and his countenance fell. And the Lord said unto Cain, Why art thou wroth? and why is thy countenance fallen?*

I mean: Davis and I each brought forth our offerings.

In our household, our mother was Lord.

Davis and I lived together as adults only once, and for only ten months, not too long after we first came out to each other when we were in our twenties. "I think we have some things to talk about," Davis told me on the phone one afternoon, proposing that we meet for lunch at a coffee shop downtown. I had graduated from college the year before; I was preparing to enter a one-year program that would certify me as a teacher. As for Davis: He had dropped in and out of community college at least a few times, and now he was repairing a broken-down U.S. mail truck he'd bought at government auction, outfitting it with an old mattress, a camp stove, and an eight-track stereo he'd gotten cheap from

138

a dealer friend who'd gotten busted. He'd soon be lighting out for San Francisco, he told me, and once he got there, he wouldn't be coming back.

By then, Davis and I hadn't been close in years, at least not since our father's death. That was when I began turning him into the darker brother, I suppose, the one to whom I assigned the feelings I myself was afraid to feel. Sometimes at night, when I saw him sitting alone in his room, for instance, pasting old photos of our father into his scrapbook, I judged him as being morose and pathetic, as if none of his feelings had anything to do with me. *What's the matter with him? I thought. Why can't he act like a normal person? Thank God we're nothing alike.* When I saw him at school, sitting alone in the lunchroom or coming down a corridor toward me, I quickly turned away, hating what I saw as his dazed helplessness and his sodden, stuttering sorrow. Other times, I felt anger and envy toward him, for I feared that his plain grief was more authentic than my own, which expressed itself largely in vague aches and anxious, giddy outbursts. At night, I sat with my mother at the dining room table long after Davis excused himself, the two of us discussing him as if he were our troubled child. "I'm concerned about his performance in school," I told her. "He isn't applying himself. He doesn't even have friends."

Not that these things weren't true of me, too,

of course—though I was hoping that no one would see them. By high school, I had concluded that it was Davis—with his unkempt clothes and thick glasses, his bad grades and stammering awkwardness, which I saw then only as a wearying, stuporous timidity—who was responsible for my having failed to achieve my own popularity, the lost cause I was in those days always advancing. I wanted people to like me. I wanted it so badly, in fact, that it could have been carved right into my tombstone: DO YOU LIKE ME? DO YOU LIKE ME YET? R.I.P.

But something changed between Davis and me the afternoon we met downtown for lunch, sitting in a small vinyl booth, facing one another. Davis leaned forward as he talked. When we were in high school, he confided, he'd sometimes taken our mother's Impala and driven downtown to have sex with a Korean man he'd met in a park, an accountant who lived in a boardinghouse near Dupont Circle. He and the man never really spoke, Davis said; nothing was exchanged between them, nothing but sex, which was hurried and guilty, and which provided only the most momentary relief, followed by Davis's long drive back to our house in the suburbs, listening to the call-in shows on stations our mother had preprogrammed on her car radio. He'd also had sex a few times with a popular boy, he said, a football player he'd occasionally brought back to our house while our mother was working, offering him some beer or a little marijuana, though the boy never acknowledged him afterward, not even with a quick nod if they happened to pass one another in the hallway the next day at school.

As for me, I had less to tell: I had fallen in love with a straight man, not for the first time, and I couldn't understand why he wouldn't love me back. As I spoke, I gestured with my hands for emphasis, as I always did, even though my mother had told me she found my behavior "a bit theatrical."

I noticed that my brother was staring at me.

"What?" I asked him.

"It's your hands," he said. "It's the way you move your hands. It's beautiful."

"Oh," I said. Because I thought it was shameful. Because it was something I was always trying to stop.

A few months later, Davis took off for San Francisco in his mail truck, and six months after that, he was back again—he hadn't even made it across the Rockies. When his truck broke down in Atlanta, he somehow managed to get it repaired, he said, but then it broke down in New Orleans, and then again in Austin, where he ran out of money. When he phoned our mother from Austin, he told her he hadn't eaten anything but dog food and saltines for almost a week, and now his teeth were hurting him, too, and when he went to the clinic, the dentist told him he wouldn't even look at him unless he paid in cash up front.

"Can you cable me money for the dentist?" he asked. "Can you send it overnight by Western Union? Bill and I really need to eat."

"Who's Bill?" our mother inquired. "Who's Bill? I haven't heard of this Bill before."

"I met Bill in Atlanta," he said. "We're living together. In the truck."

"All right, all right," she said. "I don't need to know more. But I want you to tell me you're coming back. Just come back home and be yourself. Can you promise me that?"

On that condition, she cabled the money. And a few weeks later, there was Davis, back on her doorstep. But there was no Bill along with him. Bill had bailed in Memphis, Davis later told me, as soon as he met someone else.

I told my brother we could share an apartment. After all, he needed a place and so did I, having just recently returned from my teacher training to take a part-time job at a local school.

While Davis found work of his own, as an aide at a group home for retarded adults, I found us an inexpensive place in Dupont Circle, two rooms on the first floor of a dilapidated row house, with a small kitchen, from which a steep flight of rickety stairs descended to the basement. The basement was dark and windowless, with pipes and electrical wiring running along its low ceiling. It had once served as a coal bin.

That was where Davis lived.

He lived in the basement, along with a battered chest of drawers, a bookcase, and the mattress he'd salvaged from his mail truck. When I first showed him the apartment, suggesting we split both the space and the cost, he said he'd have to live in the basement, since he was too broke to pay even a third of the rent. He didn't mind the basement too much, he claimed, not even with its dampness.

I lived upstairs, grading papers by a sunny window. I had a Boston fern. A few spider plants in glazed pots.

On weekends, I had friends to dinner, straight friends from college or teaching colleagues whom I felt I should impress. Chicken breasts in white wine, with tarragon. Steak au poivre, with a mustard sauce. Thick stalks of white asparagus.

When he was home, Davis came upstairs to join us, whether or not I'd invited him. I tried to control the conversation, embarrassed by his recitations of plots from *Star Trek* and his earnest lectures on the prophecies of Nostradamus or the beauty of Buckminster Fuller's geodesic domes or the dire necessity for zero population growth. At the same time, I feared he'd go off at any moment on to what I considered to be one of his hectoring monologues, particularly if he managed to turn the topic to homosexuality, a subject I was often trying to avoid, at least around straight people, whom I imagined myself as needing to protect. "What you fail to realize," he might suddenly announce to the dinner table, "is the specific nature of homosexual oppression, which has a *name*: It is called *self-hatred*. You fail to see that it's society that requires us to hate ourselves—that it is society and not people like me who need *immediate* and *interventional* psychiatric attention!"

"Yes," the guests would warily assent. "Yes, quite so," they would say. "You make your case well."

After dinner, he sometimes took them down to the basement to show off his handiwork. He had already covered two of the sooty brick walls with plasterboard; he was planning to drape an old parachute from the ceiling to hide the plumbing pipes and rough wooden beams.

"Nice job, nice job," the guests would say as they climbed back up the stairs toward the kitchen, where I was scraping dishes into the garbage. But no one ever asked me the question I both feared and expected—why my brother was living down-stairs in a dark basement while I was living upstairs, in rooms with windows overlooking a sunny street. And what would I have said if someone had asked? That it was simply a question of money and nothing more?

Once the guests left, I relaxed a bit. Alone with my brother, I began to regard him not as a social liability but as someone quite likable, as someone who was not so much unpredictable as he was original and bold. At these times, I saw him in the role of the older brother I wanted, the one who might guide me safely into a sexual life I both desired and feared. Once we were alone, Davis and I would smoke a little dope together. He'd drop a Quaalude, maybe two. If it was a Saturday night, we'd drive across town to hit the gay discos that had just opened in an old warehouse district. The Lost and Found. Pier Nine. Grand Central.

Inside the disco, I stood alone at the bar and watched Davis talk and flirt with guys he'd met while cruising at other gay bars and dance clubs. He had a way of holding his beer bottle in one hand—low, and close to his hip—that made him look dashing and sexy and languorous, standing there in his Levi's and denim jacket.

I hadn't remembered him as being so beautiful. When had it happened? And how had I failed for so long to see it? For years I had seen him only as the abjected one. But now The Abject was moving across the dance floor, his shirt unbuttoned to reveal his muscled chest, his arm around another man's waist; and it was I who was standing in the corner, watching him—my handsome older brother—as he moved through a world I was afraid to enter, no matter how much I wanted to. He sometimes danced for hours, first with one man, and then another and another—"Love Train," "What's Going On," "Bang a Gong," "Walk on the Wild Side," "Killing Me Softly with His Song" . . . I watched him the whole time as he danced and danced, exuberant, tireless, laughing, beneath the pulsing strobe lights.

Invariably, I went home before him. I told myself I had papers to grade.

A few times, I was awakened in the middle of the night by the sound of him moving across the kitchen—*Shh*, he was drunkenly whispering to whomever he'd brought back with him. Then I heard two pairs of footsteps hurrying down the basement stairs.

Those nights, I lay awake, listening to him down in the basement, having sex. A few times, I tried to discern his voice from the voice of the man he'd brought home from the bar. If I could figure out which voice was Davis's, I thought, I might know how I myself sounded on the rare occasions when I had sex, because our voices were identical. Everyone said so. But whatever noise it was that I was hearing—a moan, a quick laugh, a sudden crying out—I didn't like it. It scared me, that sound of losing control.

My mother loved history. She loved best her own history, of course, her stories of growing up in one of the largest houses in Park Slope, with a Stutz-Bearcat and a chauffeur and two servants from the West Indies. But when she had to, she liked the other kind of history as well, the public kind that others can share. She liked the Civil War. The worst thing about the Civil War, she used to tell Davis and me when we were growing up, the very worst thing of all, a horror she could barely stand even to consider, was that it had turned brother against brother.

"Brother against brother!" Davis and I hooted, mimicking the things she'd said to us throughout our childhoods as we drove together out to the suburbs every other Sunday to see her. This is how we entertained ourselves, working her up into a character whom we could then deride: "Brother against brother! What a drama queen! Can you *believe* it?"

She was living then in Orchard Village, the retirement community to which she had moved with Jerry, her new husband, a childless widower she had married at the county courthouse the year before. Jerry was taciturn; for his hobby, he liked to track the infinitesimal daily shifts in interest rates on tax-free bonds and government securities, which he recorded each evening in a red spiral notebook. The night my mother first met him at Post-Cana, her social club for widowed Catholics, she phoned me with breathless excitement: "He has haunted eyes," she said, "like Glenn Ford." But as soon as I met him, I saw she was wrong: His eyes weren't haunted; they were dead.

This particular Sunday, as we drove out to Orchard Village, Davis sat beside me in the passenger seat of my VW, getting stoned. "You want some?" he asked, offering me a hit from the hash pipe he'd just rigged from aluminum foil.

147

"Not me," I said. I had been stoned only once in my mother's presence. The whole time I'd felt as if my skin were transparent and she could see right through me.

Davis fiddled with the car radio, unable to find a song he wanted to hear. He was growing sullen, now that we were getting closer to our mother's.

"I don't know why we go there," he said, after a few miles. "You know she's never going to accept us, not the way we are. She's never accepted *me* at least, not since I came out. Don't you get sick of it?"

Did I get sick of it? Yes, most certainly. Right then, for instance, I was sick of this very topic, and I was angry at Davis for having gotten stoned. I knew from experience where this was headed. Soon he would be telling me that it was high time that I came out to her, just as he had; it was long overdue, in fact. Then he would start saying that he would be quite happy to tell her for me, if *that* was what it was going to take—after all, carpe diem.

"We are going there," I told him, "because she is our mother."

As soon as I said this, I regretted it. According to Davis, that was all I ever said: *She's our mother, she's our mother, she's our mother.*

But what else was I going to tell him? That I feared having a relationship with her that even resembled his, with its endless squabbles and quarrels and long, reproachful silences? After all,

148

I was the younger brother, which meant I'd had more than ample opportunity to observe their enmeshed and ferocious battles and, from observing them, I had learned how better to soothe our mother's fears and sudden rages, for which, in exchange, I received from her something that felt like approval—this was my famous "instinct for survival," I suppose. And even though I'd been only an observer, I had never once been able to forget—as neither had Davis—what had happened the first time he was arrested for selling marijuana, when he was eighteen, and our mother sent him away to live with relatives and then refused to allow him to return, despite his repeated entreaties, despite his long, wrenching letters, quoting from Henry David Thoreau and Martin Luther King and Oscar Wilde's *De Profundis*, begging her over and over to let him come home. From witnessing what had transpired between them, I had most certainly drawn different conclusions than Davis about how best to handle our mother. But I had nonetheless absorbed the same stark lesson as he: From our mother's house, it was possible to be banished.

Why then should I risk myself by coming out to her, I reasoned, if that seemed the possible price? I had lived a long time in what felt like her light.

When we arrived at the entrance to Orchard Village, we stopped at the guardhouse, as was required, to explain whom we had come to visit.

The guard eyed us with suspicion, then consulted a roster and waved us on. Soon we were parking at the curb in front of our mother's retirement cottage, and she was standing at her front door, waving.

"Hello!" she called out. "Hello! Hello! Long time, no see."

"Mom, it's only been two weeks," Davis told her.

Her brief kiss. The dry scent of her carnation talc, matching perfume. A glimpse of her husband seated at the table in the dining nook behind her, clipping articles from the newspaper.

"How about something to eat?" she asked Davis and me. "How about some sandwiches? I could make you boys some sandwiches—if you'd like some, I mean."

"No," Davis told her.

Then it began: the standard Sunday afternoon visit. The Ceremonial Visit, as Davis called it when speaking just to me. The Deep Bowing Down to the Hour of Tedium. The Royal Presentation of the Chitchat.

It started well enough. Jerry joined us, at our mother's insistence; we all sat together in the living room in upholstered chairs banked with needle-point pillows. Our mother went first, recounting a rambling story about living in a studio apartment in Greenwich Village during the war, and how she and her girlfriends had only one pair of silk stockings to share among themselves, which

150

they did without fighting, granting the highest priority of use to those who had dates with active-duty soldiers. She asked how my job was going, and whether or not I liked teaching, and if I had any students who showed talent or promise. She asked Davis and me if there was anything we needed to take back to our apartment with us, some canned fruit, maybe, some pears or peaches in heavy syrup, because she'd picked up some extras on special at the store. Occasionally, Jerry interjected some stray remark about his wartime experiences as an enlisted man in the U.S. Navy, stationed in the South Pacific.

"You know, I have a job, too," Davis interrupted. "In case anyone wants to hear about it."

I had noticed Davis was growing edgier and edgier the longer we sat there. To compensate, I had already adopted a voice of resolute cheer, responding with anxious eagerness to whatever anyone said, no matter how trivial: *Goodness! Is that right? I had no idea! Now when did that happen? No, I hadn't heard. That's so interesting! I can hardly believe it.*

"All right," our mother suddenly said, looking at Davis. "I would have asked about your job. If you had given me half a chance, I mean."

I trained my eyes on the front window, through which I could see a Latino groundsman mowing their lawn.

As for Jerry, he was still in the Pacific: "The thing no one seems to realize," he was saying, "is that we would never have won the war without the Aussies."

"Is that right?" I said to him. "I had no idea."

But something had already broken.

Davis turned toward Jerry and looked at him directly. "I hear there are a lot of gays in the navy," Davis said. "Now why is that? Did you know any gays during the war?"

"Oh, Christ," our mother said. "Here we go again. Just tell me one thing. Just one little thing: Why must everything always come back to *that*?"

"To what?" Davis said. "Come back to what? Just say the word. Just say it *once*. I dare you."

"No," she said. "I don't have to say anything. I just want to know why you have to make it such an obsession. That's what it is with you, you know—an *obsession*."

"An obsession?" Davis said. "Is that what you said? An obsession?"

She turned to me, as if only the two of us were sitting there. "Maybe *you* can explain it," she said. "Maybe you can help me figure out this one thing: *Why* is he always talking and talking and talking about it? *Why?* What does he want? Is he doing it for attention?"

Oh, right, I thought. *Of course. For attention.*

After all, that was her prevailing theory of his life: Whatever he did, he did for attention. That was why he'd gotten bad grades in school and why he'd gotten arrested; that was why he'd dropped out of community college and why he'd let himself

152

run out of money in Austin. It was all for attention. For as far back as I could recall, she had had a way of speaking of attention that made even the slightest desire for it seem suspect and pernicious. Attention? What a joke! What a ridiculous thing to want! Who in his right mind would ever admit to wanting something the world simply wasn't prepared to give?

That is: She herself had often hungered for attention that had not come to her, even as a child; now she had learned to guard herself by rejecting such hunger as weakness and by replacing it with what she considered to be her pride.

But did I say any of this? Of course not. I was the good son—unlike Cain, I wasn't known for my back talk.

Besides, it was already too late for that.

"You want to know what an obsession is?" Davis was shouting. "*This* is an obsession!" he said, pointing to the breakfront where she displayed her collection of cut glass. "This is your obsession, an obsession with things that are *fragile* and *breakable*, an obsession with things that no one's even allowed to *touch*!"

"No," she said. "That is what happens to be called 'cut glass.'"

"Oh, right," he said. "Cut glass. Your precious cut glass. But let me say this—what I am trying to talk to you about is *not* an obsession. It is me. It is who I am. It is my life."

Right then I saw him look toward me for a

moment, almost pleadingly, as if asking me to step in and defend him—or perhaps even to stop him.

I didn't know what to say. After all, I wasn't the one who'd wanted to talk about any of this to begin with—it hadn't been *my* choice. I broadcast him a quick look that meant *Don't. Don't you dare. Don't even think of saying one single word about me.*

And then I saw the argument drain out of him. His shoulders sagged, and his face drew shut, like a door that had just been quietly closed.

"Okay," he said. "All right. I guess it's time that we got going. I guess it's getting kind of late."

"But what about coffee?" our mother said. "Don't you want some coffee while you're here?"

"No," he said. "No, thank you. No coffee. Not for me. Not today."

"Jerry," she said, "tell them to stay for coffee. Tell them you'd like to have some coffee, too. Tell them they don't have to go yet."

But Jerry just glanced at Davis and me, presenting us with a brief, thin-lipped smile. It was getting close to five o'clock, the hour when he liked to be served his supper. Each night he started with the same thing, a mound of small-curd cottage cheese draped with a few canned peach slices. He didn't like his dinner ever to be late.

"Mom, it's all right," I said. "We really do have to go. I have papers to grade."

"I know you boys are busy," she said. "I know

154

you've got places you need to go. But I wish you'd take something with you. Isn't there something you need?"

"No, we're fine," I told her.

"Davis, what about you?" she said. "Isn't there something you need? Some canned fruit, maybe . . ."

"No," he said. "There is nothing I need."

And then: the Ceremony of Good-Byes, as Captured in the Pier Mirror in the Foyer.

"Good-bye," she said. "Good-bye. Be careful. Drive safely. Come back soon. Come back. Come back."

As soon as Davis and I were back in the car, he turned to me. I was pretty sure I knew what he was going to say: He was going to accuse me of having deserted him, and maybe I deserved it.

But instead he just sighed and leaned back against the headrest. "Let's get drunk," he said. "It's time to get drunk. Let's get drunk now."

"Where?" I asked.

"Dolly's," he said. "I would say this is definitely a Dolly's kind of day."

Why not? I thought—it seemed like a good idea. Dolly's was one of his favorite hangouts, a country-and-western drag bar next to the Trailways bus station downtown. It was always cheering, at the least, to watch the drag queens with their towering haystack hairdos, as they lip-synched to Tammy Wynette and Loretta Lynn and Minnie Pearl and Patsy Cline. Occasionally, a Diana Ross or a

Carmen Miranda would amble onto the small plywood stage, perhaps as a joke, and the guys in the bar would go wild, banging their beer cans against the tables, although whether they did so in pleasure or disapproval, I never could tell.

But what I'd told my mother was true—I did have papers to grade, a set of themes my students had written on subjects taken from life; I'd promised to return them quickly. I told Davis that I'd drop him at Dolly's and come back to meet him later, as soon as I was finished, in a couple of hours.

It was almost four hours later when I got back to Dolly's—the papers had taken longer than expected. But as soon as I came through the door of the bar, I saw Davis was still there, sitting at a table in the corner with some guy I'd never seen before.

"Hey, brother!" he called out when he spotted me. "Hey, brother, get over here!"

I waved at him through the crowd. I was wondering if he was drunk already. There was something forlorn about him, a homeless quality, as if he'd been waiting for me all those hours because he wasn't sure where else he had to go.

I made my way toward him through the smoke-filled bar, through the noisy crush of men in flannel shirts and Levi's, some of them huddled together in small groups, drinking cans of beer, while others—the ones who'd come alone, it seemed—stood sentry along the walls. Onstage, a drag queen was lip-synching to "Stand by Your Man," although each time she extended her opera-gloved arms toward the audience, enacting what she took to be some particularly dramatic portion of the song, I saw that her mouth was moving slightly out of time with the music.

When I got to the other side of the bar, I took the seat Davis had been saving for me beside him. "Hey, brother, have some beer," he said. "I bought a pitcher. Why don't you join me?"

He lifted the pitcher of beer and began to pour me a glass, but, as he did so, his arm suddenly drooped and jerked as if the muscle had gone slack, and the beer spilled across the table and started dripping down onto the floor. There was something wobbly about him, as if the synapses in his brain weren't firing in quite the right order.

"Hey, man, watch it!" said the guy who was sharing his table.

Davis started blotting up the spilled beer with some napkins. "I'm sorry," he said. "I'm sorry, I'm sorry. There, I said it, okay? *I'm sorry*."

"Fuck you," the guy said as he got up to leave, taking his beer glass with him.

I moved my chair closer to Davis's. "Are you all right?" I asked.

"Yeah, sure," he said. "I'm wonderful."

I could see that wasn't true. "Have you taken something?" I asked him. "You don't seem right."

"'Ludes," he said. "I took a few Quaaludes. Is that all right? Maybe you should try a few, brother."

I knew what he was telling me, and not for the first time: I was too uptight for my own good. He had told me more than once how Quaaludes made you feel relaxed and vivid and sexual, all at the same moment, but I resisted because I wasn't sure that was a combination I was really ready to feel.

It seemed best to say nothing. Davis pulled his chair closer to mine and put an arm around my shoulders. For a while, we just sat like that, watching the drag performer together. To someone who didn't know us, I kept thinking, we probably looked like a couple.

"I guess I fucked up," Davis said after some minutes. "This afternoon at Mom's, I mean. Go ahead and say it. Go ahead, since you probably want to: *You're a royal fuckup, Davis, that's you . . .*"

"That's not true," I said, though I wasn't sure I meant it. When I looked at him, I saw that his face was flushed from the beer and Quaaludes mixed together.

He moved even closer, then waved his free hand toward a group of men standing at the bar. "You see any guys you like?" he asked.

"I don't know," I told him. When I looked at the men at the bar, I felt uncertain, just as I always did in gay clubs, since I found it so hard to distinguish between my anxiety and my desire.

Then Davis leaned forward, as if to whisper something in my ear. "You know," he said, "you're a good-looking guy. Do you know that? Do you know you're a good-looking guy?" I could feel his warm breath on my face as he spoke.

"Oh, thank you," I said. "You are, too." I was using my pleasant voice, the one I always used when I was nervous.

"That's not what I meant," he said, his voice slightly slurred. "I mean you're *really* a good-looking guy. I mean—come on, you know—haven't you ever *thought* about it, even for just a minute? You know, you and me, the two of us, maybe going back to our place together . . ."

For a moment, I didn't believe what I was hearing. He can't possibly mean what he seems to be saying, I told myself.

Then his words suddenly assembled themselves into some order, and the question he had just posed struck me with blunt force: *Haven't you ever thought about it?* Yes, sure, of course, maybe I had—maybe for a moment, maybe once or twice at the most. Maybe I'd even thought of it a few times, those nights I'd been awakened by the sound of him down in the basement having sex— but it was wrong to think of it for more than a moment, and it was even wronger still to speak . . .

I felt Davis's hand settling on my knee. "What's the matter?" he whispered.

I jumped. "What's the matter?" I said, my voice surprising me in its shrillness. "Are you really asking me that? It's *you*. You're what's the matter. What's the matter is *you!*"

I pushed back from the table; I pushed back

hard and stood and started moving quickly toward the door. And as to what happened next? Don't even ask me if the bar I was moving through was still crowded or noisy or smoke-filled, or whether or not a drag queen was performing one of her numbers onstage. I don't know. I don't know. I just don't remember.

Here's what I do remember: For three days, I stayed at a friend's house, afraid to return to the apartment even for a change of clothes. I couldn't imagine how I'd ever live there again, not with my brother in the basement below me, moving around at night, making sounds I didn't want to hear. It was as if I had cast some part of myself down in the basement with him, and now that I had done so, I wanted it to remain down there in the dark forever, without even the slightest chance that it might one day climb back up those same stairs to greet me.

On the fourth day, I made myself go back. I found Davis sitting in my bedroom, reading a book by the window—a book about space travel, if I remember correctly.

"Where have you been?" he asked, looking up from what he was reading. "I was worried about you. I thought maybe you'd gone off to trick with someone."

"I have to talk to you," I said. "We have to talk about Dolly's."

"Oh, Dolly's," he said, closing the book and

setting it on the small table beside him. "I'm not sure what I remember. I remember having a few beers. I remember taking some 'ludes. But after that—I don't even know how I got back here. I was in a blackout, I guess."

"A blackout?" I said. "Are you serious?"

"Yeah, a real blackout," he said. "I've never had a real blackout before."

I thought to press harder. I wasn't sure whether or not to believe him.

But at the same time, I felt relieved. After all, why bring up something so troubling and difficult when he claimed not even to remember it? Perhaps if I said nothing more, I thought, it would be over and done with. In fact, it might in time become something that had never really happened at all. Yes, that was it: It was just something that had happened to me and me alone—and since that was the case, wasn't it up to me as to how real it had to become or how much of it I would even need to remember?

In the weeks that followed, I kept telling myself that nothing had changed between Davis and me, not really. After all, wasn't it true, what we had told ourselves as children—that no matter what, we would always have each other as brothers?

And then, a few months later, I suddenly packed up and moved away. I decided to return to graduate school, this time in the Midwest, 1,200 miles from anywhere I had ever lived. I was thinking to write a doctoral dissertation on homosexuality in

American cinema, since I seemed so much better at theory than practice. Maybe my dissertation would be published as a book, I thought, and attract some favorable attention, and maybe even win an award or two, as something notable and scholarly. And if that happened, I imagined, I would never have to come out to my mother, at least not directly, not in so many words. Instead, I would have discovered an alchemical process capable of converting something shameful into an irreproachable achievement, an offering that I could set before my mother and that she would then be compelled to recognize as something prestigious and worthy, at least in the eyes of the world. *And the Lord had respect unto Abel . . .*

Not that I ever wrote such a book, of course—and not that I even finished grad school, for that matter. Not that I would have given her the pleasure.

As for Davis: A few weeks after my departure, he found a new roommate, a scrawny Vietnam vet who had just come out but who'd already developed the habit of referring to himself only in the third person as "Miss Kitty Carlisle." It was Miss Kitty Carlisle who told me they had transformed what had once been my bedroom into a sunny living room that they could share.

Occasionally that fall, Davis and I spoke on the phone late at night, although never for more than just a few minutes. I complained to him about graduate school, the dismal earnestness of my fellow students; I complained about the Midwest and the inane pleasantries one had to endure in living there.

Davis said he was happy. Or happy enough. He had his friends. A few lovers.

He was given a promotion at the group home for retarded adults where he worked; he was now the supervisor of dinner preparations, in addition to being the driver of the van for the disabled.

He said he was thinking of taking a second job, this one checking IDs at the door of a new gay bar that had opened in Dupont Circle. He needed money.

He needed money, he said, because he'd begun developing a whole new plan for achieving his life-long dream of moving to San Francisco. He felt sure he was going to make it this time. He was planning to buy a used car, as soon as he was able. He was planning to cut back on his drinking.

And then my mother phoned to tell me that Davis had been arrested again, this time for having sex with a man in a park at night. "Maybe he keeps getting into trouble because he thinks I'll come to his rescue," she said. "Maybe this time I should just let him sit there."

But I have already told you that story.

So let me tell you this instead: Counting forward from the night I left him at Dolly's, my brother had only nine more years to live.

As always, there were still a few key facts the future had yet to disclose.

For instance, the fact that I would find myself sitting here one day without him, as I am now, attempting to remember the same things I'd once urged myself to forget. Or the fact that I would want to tell someone that a long time ago, when we were children, our mother dressed us as twins.

That I sometimes crawled into his upper bunk at night to fall asleep beside him. That "peanut butter" meant "I'm sorry." That "applesauce" meant "Laugh!"

What can I say of the years that remained to my brother—or of all the years that have passed since his death? Shall I tell you his life was difficult? That he seldom had a regular pay-check? That he was poor and had only a lockbox under his bed in which to store bits of cash and never so much as a bank account or a credit card? That he was beloved by his close circle of friends, who found him smart and garrulous and loyal?

At first, in the years right after his arrest in the park, his life was on the upswing. At his trial, the judge sentenced him to a year's probation, assuring him that his court record would eventually be expunged, on the condition—as the judge put it— that he comport himself in the meantime with "accepted standards of decent behavior." That spring, he and Miss Kitty Carlisle moved to a new apartment, where he now occupied a sunny bedroom overlooking a garden that blazed all summer with crape myrtles and gladioli.

The next fall, he was admitted to a local college, aided by a city grant designed to help repeat offenders; on the basis of his "life experience," he was awarded sufficient credits to become a junior. When he graduated two years later, our mother attended the ceremony, carrying her instant camera so she could snap a photo of him wearing a mortarboard and tassel.

She gave him money, which he used to study American Sign Language at Gallaudet College, with the idea of becoming an interpreter. He met Paul, the deaf man who became his lover, and when Paul moved in with him and Miss Kitty Carlisle, Davis hooked their phone to a TTY and rigged some wiring so that a light flashed when anyone rang the doorbell.

And then the life he had begun to make for himself slowly started to unravel. No one, not even he, saw it coming, I suppose. Who could say why?

He resumed his drinking. He started cutting morning classes at Gallaudet because he was hungover. He fell behind in his share of the rent and borrowed money from Paul. The next year, when the time came for him to take his exam for certification as an official ASL interpreter, he refused, claiming that the exam was meaningless and so poorly made as to be rigged against those like himself who were fluent.

He and our mother renewed their old arguments. She accused him of using drugs again. He accused her of being cold. When she threatened to stop paying for his health insurance, as she had been doing for years, he refused to return her phone calls.

Then Paul moved out, taking with him everything he and Davis had purchased together, even the pair of ceramic lamps Davis had smashed one night while he and Paul were fighting.

For a while, Davis worked as an office temp, but he inevitably fought with his employers. For money, he taught occasional classes in the basement of his building for gay men who wanted to learn a bit of ASL, a few signs to use when flirting with deaf guys in bars: CAN I BUY YOU A BEER? WHERE DO YOU LIVE? WHAT KIND OF SEX ARE YOU INTO?

Increasingly, he spurned the hearing world as much as possible; more and more, his friends were men who were deaf or profoundly hard of hearing. Often when strangers stopped him on the sidewalk to ask for the time or directions, he shrugged his shoulders and pointed an index finger to his ear to indicate he couldn't hear.

He did odd jobs. He cleaned apartments. Occasionally, he worked weekend nights at the Chesapeake House, a gay dive where he go-go danced on the beer-slicked bar for the tips that men tucked into his G-string. It was there he was arrested the third time, for selling amphetamines and Quaaludes to an undercover cop who'd approached him in the men's room.

And how do I know these things?

Because I saw him once a year at least, each

time I came back east to visit our mother and Jerry in Orchard Village, where they sat at their dining room table night after night, bickering over their household budget or the relative merits of freeze-dried versus regular instant coffee. Each time I went downtown to visit Davis, our mother sought to recruit me as her emissary, asking me to return with a report on his drinking.

I did as she requested. And why not? I was still more my mother's keeper than my brother's, at least back then.

The last time I visited him in his apartment, I sat beside him on the sofa, working the conversation toward the inevitable: "Mom's worried about your drinking," I finally said. "She wants to know how much you drink."

"Tell her whatever you want," he said. He picked up his glass of vodka and drained it in just a few gulps. Then he looked at me directly. "Just tell her you've never even seen me touch so much as a drop."

The next time I saw him was a hot August afternoon ten months later. I was doing a few errands in his neighborhood, though I hadn't yet told him I was in town. I spotted him coming down the block toward me.

He looked terrible—pale and tired and sweaty, as if he had a bad summer cold or the flu. His appearance scared me, and for a moment I considered turning away as if I hadn't seen him. I remember thinking, *Thank God we're nothing alike.*

"Hey, brother!" he said when he spotted me. He rapidly signed the words as he spoke them, as he always did.

"Hey," I said back.

I just stood there. And then I suddenly found myself telling him I was in a hurry, sorry, I didn't have time to talk. I left him there, standing on the sidewalk. *Don't turn around*, I told myself.

He died a month later of a drug overdose. He was thirty-five.

It was Miss Kitty Carlisle who found his body. When he got home from the dance club he'd been to the night before, he noticed there was water all over the bathroom floor; then he noticed a trail of water leading down the hallway. He knocked on Davis's door; when there was no answer, he went in and found Davis lying dead on his bed with his clothes soaking wet. Miss Kitty Carlisle said he could tell right away that Davis had been dead for hours.

Davis had been "partying with friends," someone who knew him told me later, though this person kept insisting he hadn't been there. He told me that everyone had been smoking dope and snorting coke, except Davis, who had been drinking vodka and shooting heroin. When Davis first showed signs of an overdose—he kept nodding out, his breathing was shallow and labored—his friends had tried to revive him by carrying him to the bathtub and plunging him into cold water. When that didn't work, they carried him back down the hall to his room and placed him on his bed. It was there that he died, a police detective later surmised, after nothing that the mattress had been soaked with urine as well as water. In any case, as soon as they placed him on his bed, his friends pulled down the blinds and fled the apartment, leaving his body behind.

"The people who were there that night must have been deaf," my mother said to me after she learned what had happened. "I know it. They were deaf. That's why they didn't call the rescue squad. They didn't know how to use the telephone."

"That's not true," I told her. "The deaf know how to use a phone."

Then the coroner's report arrived with its unambiguous summation: "MANNER OF DEATH: ACCIDENTAL."

But even now, years later, I still have some questions of my own.

For instance: Why *didn't* anyone stop to call the police or even just an ambulance before fleeing his apartment? No one would have been required to give his real name. And even if they were all both deaf and mute, he had a TTY. How long did Davis's dead body lie there alone?

And this: Why did I run from him that night at Dolly's?

If what he proposed that night was really so unthinkable or appalling, I see now that I might have responded simply by saying no. Didn't some part of me want to go with him, to descend those basement stairs to his room?

I know that I now miss his body—the body I pressed against in sleep as a child, back when I still imagined we were sharing just one body between us.

Why did I leave him standing on the sidewalk, alone, the last time I saw him? Why did I tell myself not even to turn and look back? Was I so afraid to see myself reflected in him, to glimpse those parts of myself that I most feared and thus repudiated as belonging only to him—those parts of me that were angry and desirous, rebellious and sexual and scared?

And as for Cain and Abel, who were themselves divided: I know what the Torah teaches, that separation and distinction are the basis of all creation, that heaven is distinct from earth, just as light is distinct from darkness and the firmament distinct from the seas—*Baruch Hamavdil Bein Kodesh l'Chol*. But why did the Lord differentiate the two brothers and set them apart?

Was Abel's offering really the more deeply meant, as some Midrash commentaries suggest? *And Abel, he also brought of the firstlings of his flock and the fat thereof.* Each brother gave what he could, at least as I now see it. Who could blame Cain for the hurt and anger he felt when the Lord showed to his offering no regard? *He was very wroth, and his countenance fell . . .*

Was it the Lord who rended them asunder? You are the good son; you, the bad.

I was Cain and Abel both, as was my brother.

It is more than a decade since Davis's death. But at night I sometimes find myself studying his old photos. I am still trying to determine how slight or strong the resemblance was between us.

I suppose I have an answer each morning when I look at myself in the mirror. In middle age, I have grown more and more to resemble him, as if time itself were whittling away all differences— although, of course, I'm the older brother now.

I suppose I have an answer each time I hear myself on a tape recorder—*Davis!* I sometimes think, because our voices really were identical. A few times, when I've heard myself moan or cry out while having sex, I've thought of that voice I heard down in the basement years ago.

Perhaps I even had my answer the autumn afternoon my mother and I scattered Davis's ashes a few weeks after his death. That day, there were still yet months to come before I found myself at last willing to risk her displeasure by coming out to her, sitting face-to-face at her dining room table.

We were scattering his ashes atop my father's grave at Arlington National Cemetery. I was irritated with my mother, because I had wanted to fly Davis's ashes to San Francisco and release them there, in the bay beside the city he had so long dreamed of but never seen. But she wouldn't hear of it. She said she couldn't bear to think of him as being so far away from home forever.

"Hurry," she told me, as we knelt in the grass, emptying the small wooden box that held Davis's "cremains," as the man at the mortuary had called them. She was afraid a guard or a groundsworker would spot us, since what we were doing was against military graveyard regulations.

We said a quick "Hail Mary," then drove back to Orchard Village in silence—I had promised her I'd come back to her house for lunch. "Don't you want a sandwich before you head back home?" she'd kept asking me that morning. "Won't you let me make you a sandwich before you go?"

When we got to her house, I headed for the bathroom so I could be alone for a moment. On the way, I passed the door to the den, where Jerry sat working at his desk, copying figures into his spiral notebook.

"Hey, come here a moment," he said, looking up. "I want to ask you a question."

"What?" I said, pausing in the doorway.

He set down his pencil and turned toward me. "It's a personal question," he said. "I hope you don't mind if it's personal."

A *personal* question? I thought. A *personal* question? *Poor, befuddled Jerry,* I thought—*always at least a few steps behind the game.* After all, he wasn't what one would call a conversationalist. What had he ever wanted to know that could possibly have been considered "personal"?

"Okay," I told him. "Shoot."

"It's something I've wondered about," he said.

"I mean, let me ask you—I just want your opinion. Do you think Davis was a real gay? Or did he do it for attention?"

For a moment, I just stood there, staring. For the first time, I could feel something fierce and hard building suddenly inside me, a rage I had always imagined as belonging only to Davis. I glared at Jerry. *There he sits,* I thought, *with his buzz cut and dead eyes and Twist-o-Flex watchband: the marks of the beast.*

"What the hell do you mean?" I exploded. "What the hell do you mean? Nothing you say means a thing to me. Nothing you say ever has—not one fucking word. What could you possibly mean by a term like 'a real gay'?"

Right then we were both startled by my outburst. Everything was quiet. I could hear my mother unwrapping dishes in the kitchen, and I wondered if she'd heard what I had just said. I suddenly felt ashamed of the tone I had taken toward her husband.

Then Jerry leaned forward. "You know what I mean," he said. "You know—a *real gay,* like you."

THE UNIVERSE, CONCEALED

*For Ellen Geist,
in memory of her son, Jesse*

My friend Helen and I are rowing a boat on Eagle Lake. It's almost dusk, but Helen is wearing her swimsuit because she's working on a tan. She has brought along her bottle of Hawaiian Tropic suntan oil and a Panasonic cassette player made of cheap white plastic, like a teenage girl's. As we row, we listen to *The Torah Tapes*, which Helen has secured from a Hasidic man who runs a shop on Eastern Parkway in Brooklyn. He also sells special Yahrzeit candles, she says, although she prefers the ordinary kind that come in blue paper wrappers, available in regular grocery stores. She says they remind her of the Dixie cups of ice cream her father bought her when she was a girl in Livingston, New Jersey.

"Be neither sad nor regretful," says Rabbi Ezekiel Stollman. Rabbi Stollman's our invisible passenger, the one whose voice we strain to hear when the Panasonic's batteries are running low. On *The Torah Tapes*, he speaks in a kind of up-and-down chanting.

He says that sadness is arrogance and vanity. The things that sadden us are actually blessings, he says, coming to us from a universe that's concealed.

While Rabbi Stollman talks, I feel the rhythm of rowing—the bending forward, and then the long leaning back, pulling the oars through water—as a kind of secret davening. Helen sits across from me, adjusting her swimsuit's straps. "You think I'm getting too much sun?" she asks.

For several days now, since coming to the Eagle Lake Lodge and Cottages, where we plan to spend a week, we've been making a list of the things we would see if the concealed universe were suddenly and astonishingly revealed to us. At the top of the list, we have written "UV rays."

Beneath that we have written "Joshua," the name of Helen's twelve-year-old son, who died a year ago, and then the names of my friends who have died—Jim, Edward Marcellus, Larry, George, Darnell, Allen, Ricardo, Stanley, Paul, Jaime, Billy, Eduardo, and, most recently, Francisco.

Helen says we should make a list of the things we hope will remain concealed forever. At the top of that list, she says, she'll put the cotton prosthesis she was given after her mastectomy, not long before Josh was killed. On a third list, a list of things that are generally concealed but which we believe might be revealed to us with a minimum of effort, if we put our minds to it, we plan to write "penises."

It's not surprising that we should take an interest in men's zippers, says Helen, since we're both descended from tailors who labored long hours in sweatshops. As for us: We labor in an editorial department, where our coworkers keep handing us grim full-color brochures that advertise budget holidays that they believe Helen and I should take together. And who could blame them for wanting holidays from us? Even as spiritual projects, we must be tiresome, since we spend so much of our time discussing the lives of people who are dead.

"You'll have to admit one thing," the coworker who shares my cubicle said to me one day while we were standing at a lunch counter, waiting for the clerk to bag our takeout orders. "When it comes to the dead, there are simply more of them than there are of us."

And although I saw at once the point he was driving at, as sensible and tactless as it was, I thought, *Well, yes, that's it exactly, especially when you've lost the people you've loved best—so many, in fact, that you couldn't possibly find a rental hall large enough in which to entertain them, other than the one inside your stunned but festooned head . . .*

Then I thought of my mother, who outlived almost everyone she knew, and who solved this problem like a genius simply by allowing herself to become demented. Not long after she entered the nursing home, she began calling the staff by the names of people who were dead. Once, she introduced me to the nurse as her mother. Over and over, she kept saying to the nurse, "Have you met my mother yet?" Evidently this nurse had been around the block, because she didn't miss a trick. She took one of my hands within hers and said, "Tell me, has your daughter been a good girl today?" And I thought, *Well, yes, in fact she has, and she was always more like a daughter than a mother anyway* . . .

In this way she went on for years, descending from her seven heavens—from *Machon*, with its caverns of storm and noxious smoke, and from *Araboth*, which contains the dew that will one day revive the dead—only to accuse the nurses of stealing her brassieres.

But this isn't what Rabbi Stollman has in mind when he explains the Torah, even though he too must explain the nature and meaning of the concealed universe by telling stories. In one of his stories, the ancient Jews are praying for the Creator's blessing, which they ask to come in the form of rain, since they are suffering from terrible drought and famine.

So it rains. It rains so much that their crops are destroyed. It rains so much that their beasts of burden are drowned in the fields. Then, says the rabbi, just as everything is almost lost, the Jews assemble again, with their heads bowed in submission, like beggars standing at a door. "Thank You, O Lord!" they start to pray again. "Thank You! You can stop! We've had enough blessings!"

"Make no mistake," says the rabbi. "The Creator takes an interest in human prayer."

★　　★　　★

Even here at the Eagle Lake Lodge and Cottages—
"AAA-APPROVED, SPECIAL SENIOR RATES,
IN-ROOM PHONES AND TV LOUNGE"—
there are many blessings. In the cluttered gift shop
in the lobby, for instance, there are brightly painted
iron trivets to bless the homes they'll one day deco-
rate; and seated in the pine-paneled dining room
there are numerous old ladies, most of them
widowed, who bow their Christian heads in silence
to bless their dinners. Rabbi Stollman would
be impressed, we tell ourselves, if he were to see
the old ladies as they congregate each night on the
screened-in porch in their Adirondack chairs,
praising the things the revealed world has given
them to gaze upon: hummingbirds, for instance,
and fireflies rising from the honeysuckle bushes,
and the deer that sometimes come along the
shore at night to drink from Eagle Lake.

But tonight Helen and I are sitting in the dark,
where the old ladies can't see us, down on the
dock in folding chairs. We are staring at the deep
blue line where the lake becomes sky.

"Tell me about the first time you met Francisco,"
Helen says.

I am remembering how as a child my brother,
Davis, liked to hide at night in the shrubs by our
front porch. When someone walked by, he would
whisper, "Who goes there?"

Davis died at thirty-five of an overdose. I whisper
into the water—*Davis? Who goes there?*

But Helen wants me to tell her about Francisco,

every detail. How I still drank back then, when I was living in Germany, translating NATO manuals for the U.S. Army. And how what felt like an urge for the English language suddenly led me to the airport in Frankfurt, which led to a drunken weekend in Dublin, which led to an even longer bender in Galway, until one night I found myself propositioning a sailor who was pissing into the harbor from the edge of the quay. And how a penitential journey to the Aran Islands led to a terrified week of white-knuckled sobriety, which led to a boozy overnight ferry ride to Cherbourg, which led to a morning train to Paris, with the sun in my eyes the whole way. And how that whole journey only returned me to the sort of single room I'd been trying to escape, and how that room then led me to a run-down porno theater on rue Vivienne, where a Filipino in a white shirt was sitting in silence beside me, solemnly stroking my cock through my pants.

That was Francisco, I tell her. Almost as soon as he unfastened the buttons on my fly, I came.

This is the part of the story Helen likes best— the sticky, pre-AIDS mess I make in my drawers, a kind of "meeting cute," as she calls it, like on a sitcom. But these days, I suppose, the underwear would be marked BIOHAZARD.

She also likes the part where Francisco and I leave the dirty movie theater and go to the Cinema DeLuxe, a revival house, to see *West Side Story*, and the way we walk home later, along the Champs-Élysées, singing "I Feel Pretty." I never returned to Germany.

But as I talk I am thinking, *Helen, there are parts I have not told you, things I still conceal.* The drunken nights along the Boulevard Raspail, and the shame of my desire. The sullen fights and rages. The catacombs of tenderness, and the brittle apologies.

And the way I left him, in a drunken panic. And the way his letters kept following me back to America, saying, *Save me.* Each time I opened one, I felt as if the knife were slitting the envelope into a mouth.

"Well," he said after we slept together again, a few years later, when I was visiting Paris, "I guess we've said quite enough for ourselves already. In the old days."

Oh, I thought, *in the old days* . . . But now, if one wanted, how would one get back there? Ring the bell, *monsieur*—the green iron gate on rue de la Campagne Première. Then up five steep flights to the small room beneath the eaves where those two ghosts still live—*I love you, I love you.*

But I tell none of this to Helen. We didn't know each other's dead, so we're still able to invent them.

I tell her that I loved Francisco. I tell her it is terrible that he died alone.

I tell her it is terrible that he died in that terrible apartment, in that terrible district near the airport, north of Paris, in that squalid suburb, that sort of

180

petite Afrique to which the French consign their dark-skinned foreign workers. Terrible that his body went unclaimed for three days. Terrible—well, hardly comme il faut.

But I see Helen leaning forward in her folding chair. "It's my turn," she is saying. "I want to tell about Josh."

She leans back. "Josh told me he wanted to be a doctor when he grew up," she says. "The week before my mastectomy, he told me that he wanted to become a doctor so he could cure cancer. He even showed me that he'd gone to the public library to check out a chemistry book."

She says she can remember the book's exact title, which was *Organic Chemistry*, although it was out of date and totally useless. But of course she didn't tell this to Josh.

She liked to watch him while he read. She liked to watch him as he diligently studied *Organic Chemistry*, sitting in his straight chair at the dining room table, drinking glass after glass of ice water. He was drinking so much ice water, she says, because the first brutal heat wave of summer had just begun and the air conditioner in the living room window was broken.

All evening, Helen has been abstracted and unsettled, her voice taut with anxiety, and I can see that telling her own story isn't helping her, that it is taking Josh away from her again instead of restoring him. How could it be otherwise? Tomorrow is the first anniversary of Josh's death.

According to the Hebrew calendar, Helen has told me, Josh died in the year 5754, on Tisha B'Av, which happens also to be the solemn fast day of mourning commemorating at least eight calamitous tragedies, including the destruction of the First and Second Temples, the expulsion of the Jews from Spain, the mass suicide of the Jews of York, and the initiation of the deportation of the Jews from the Warsaw Ghetto. These, says Helen, are precisely the sort of "Orthofacts" that make one realize that Hasidism is simply a brilliant cover for obsessive-compulsive disorder, given its passion for counting and numbers. For instance, according to the *Likutei Amarim-Tanya*, the 613 organs of the soul are clothed in the 613 commandments of the Torah, which are further subdivided into 248 "organs," or positive precepts, and 365 "sinews," or prohibitions. The whole thing started with Adam, who contained 248 limbs (including parts of limbs) in his initially blameless human body.

This methodology suggests, says Helen, that all inquiries into the nature of the soul are essentially obsessive and autopsical.

But Helen herself believes in the revelatory power of numbers. For instance: Josh had an IQ of 158, which means that he was his school's brightest pupil.

He owned 323 baseball cards. Helen knows this because she counted and alphabetized them shortly after he died.

He lived—in this world, at least—for a total of 4,483 days, including three leap years.

And above all, this: The week of the third blistering heat wave—the week that her veins sclerosed from her second cycle of intravenous chemo, the week that Josh was killed—Helen yelled at him twice for not having fixed the air conditioner in the living room window. He had said he would fix the air conditioner in the living room window.

"Go ahead and yell at me if you want," Josh had answered her the first time. "You're just yelling at me because I'm the only one who's here with you now."

To prove this punishing point to her forever, the next time Helen yelled, God let Josh die.

As for that point, Helen says, it needs no proving. After all, we are sitting on this dock because he's dead.

She walks to the edge of the water. "Did I tell you what I told the Hasid in West Side Judaica the day I went to buy the *Tanya*?" she asks. "I told him I was thinking of becoming a Hasid, since I no longer trusted horoscope books. I told him I'd actually been quite a devoted reader of Linda Goodman's *Sun Signs*—at least until my son was hit by a car. I said, 'Now tell me, she was Jewish, wasn't she? You know, *Goodman*? Reform, maybe? Reconstructionist?'"

She steps back from the water. *Who goes there, in the dark . . .*

When she turns to me, her face is bloated with sorrow. "I think I want to go to the bar now," she says.

The bar is the one spot to which I won't follow her, not even tonight. But I follow her up the hill, through a stand of fir pines and past the occasional wooden cottages with porch lights that dimly illuminate bags of garbage and beach towels draped on clotheslines to dry. When we come upon the lodge, I see that the old ladies have retired for the night, their white chairs in straight rows, glowing in the dark. In the taproom window, a blue neon sign advertises GENESEE BEER.

"I can't believe you're really an alcoholic," Helen says as we cross the lawn toward the front door. "It's insane. Everyone knows that Jews can't be alcoholics."

"I'm not a Jew," I say. "I'm gay."

We separate in the lobby.

But I'm not ready to go upstairs to bed. For a while, I sit on an overstuffed sofa, its back cushions pinned with yellowing antimacassars, reading back issues of *People* and *Adirondack Life*. When I look up, I can see through the open door to the taproom; I can see Helen sitting on her barstool, her legs crossed, talking with one of the summer sportsmen who sometimes come here to drink, a man in an expensive fisherman's vest.

Because I know some things that Helen has told me, I imagine that I can see what this man cannot. I can see the way she fiddles with her lavender blouse, for instance, nervously revealing and concealing a small part of her recently reconstructed breast; and I can see the way she adjust its neckline, checking to see that it shields the small, puckered surgical scars that make her self-conscious. "Just some dents in my flesh," she told me one day, as if her creator had accidentally marked her with his thumb—*as if we were clay, as if we were dust.*

In a few months, the plastic surgeon will complete the reconstruction of the nipple, what Helen calls "the frosting on the cake."

I watch as she leans back on her barstool and laughs. She hoists her cocktail glass into the air as if making a toast.

Tomorrow at breakfast, I think, she will recount this whole thing for me. "Did you get a load of that guy?" she'll ask. "Right out of *Yankee Magazine*—or maybe L.L.Bean—what do I know from the goyim? Did you see me drinking a *gimlet*?"

"That must have been the Purple Lady in the bar last night!" she'll exclaim, speaking of herself in the third person as if she were a victim of multiple-personality disorder. She'll erase the night by working it up, by laughing at it, while we sit together at the breakfast table, spooning jam onto our English muffins.

And why should she say more? It's true: In the beginning was The Word. But sometimes, says Rabbi Stollman, an unhappy person can best work his way toward God by being silent, just as a

185

hungry person can work his way toward God by delaying his meal. I know what Helen's doing.

But when I look up again, I see that she is touching the man's hand. She has grown serious, and I can tell from the way he studies her, with a convolution of horror and sympathy—a grim expression that I can recognize, having so often received it myself—that she is telling him how Josh was crossing Eighth Avenue, turning to wave to the friend who'd just called his name: "Josh!"

How the van was speeding and quickly bearing down. How the impact. How his glasses. How he was thrown.

How he rose and stood again for a moment.

How he fell. How blood. How his blue shirt. How the sirens and the stretcher.

How it happened. The whole story.

It is time for me to go upstairs.

I turn out the light. On the way up, I stop at the refrigerator the manager has placed in the stairwell and take out my medicine. On the door of the fridge, he has hung a sign: PLEASE DATE FOOD. *Oh, no*, I think each time I see it, *God willing, I'd really rather date a man . . .*

But I suppose the other guests have already guessed at that.

I know what I would guess if I were one of them, and if I happened to open the small brown paper bag that contains the clear glass vials: "New Drug. Limited by Federal Law to Investigational Use Only. For Subcutaneous Injection."

And what would I say if one of them were to ask me? "Oh, no, dear sir or madam, certainly not *that*—not *that* disease at all, I assure you!"

Is it true, what I tell myself? That if I were pressed to say this, I'd rather stand with the dead?

I go upstairs to my room. I sit on the bed and mix the recombinant with sterile water, as the study nurse taught me, and draw the solution into the syringe. I swab my thigh with alcohol. When I'm done, I lie down.

Then it's quiet, except for an occasional loon calling from the lake. I lie still and try to masturbate. *Here is his body, silvery, like water . . . And here is what he felt like, the smooth warm chest . . . Francisco, the audible pulse at his wrist, restored . . . And he says . . .*

But it doesn't work. I turn on the bedside lamp.

I imagine Helen in the bar downstairs, feeding quarters to the jukebox, dancing with the man in the fisherman's vest. What does it matter if she prepares for Tisha B'Av not by fasting but by flirting and having a few drinks more? She's already reduced her level of happiness, as Rabbi Stollman says one must in the days preceding Tisha B'Av. Perhaps the management should post a sign by the gate to the lodge to protect the innocent from straying up our driveway: CAUTION: MOURNERS AHEAD.

For a long time, I sit awake, thumbing through a magazine, until I hear Helen coming down the

187

hallway, fumbling in her handbag as if drunk, searching for the key to her room.

The next morning, Helen doesn't come down to breakfast. I sit in the dining room, watching the old ladies as they congregate on the screened-in porch, where they'll spend their morning painting rocks to look like ladybugs and mice. Mrs. Chandra, a widow originally from Bombay, is standing among them, talking to her son Sanjit, who has come to visit her. Sanjit is slender and graceful, in a white linen shirt, not much more than twenty.

"Sanjit can stay only two days," his mother said, introducing him to Helen and me the previous morning, "because he's very busy in his business, as is proper." When he shook our hands—solemn, courteous—he looked at us directly, smiling, although as soon as I looked back at him, he quickly lowered his eyes.

"Do you think he might be gay?" I asked Helen.

"You're daydreaming," she said. She said she doubted the Diaspora was now leading Jews and queers to Eagle Lodge, ourselves excluded.

One of the widows, a straggler, stops at my table on her way from breakfast. "Where's your wife this morning?" she asks.

"Sleeping, I guess," I say.

I watch as she crosses the room toward the lobby, where she stops to check her mail at the desk. When I look back out to the porch, Mrs. Chandra and her son are gone.

I sit alone in silence, looking through an old issue of *Family Circle*. For a while, I close my eyes and attempt to imagine a white light traveling through my body, as a book on creative visualization has instructed me, through the complicated circuits of my arteries and veins, with healing warmth; and then I attempt to imagine that Francisco and I are once again sitting in the sunlight on a bench near the Orangerie . . .

But what I recall is the day I learned that Francisco had died. I was at work when I received the phone call from Paris. Seven words—that's all I said when I got the news, one word for each day of the decreation: *Oui, monsieur, je comprends, certainement, au revoir.*

I hung up. I rode the elevator down to the street and began to walk home from Hudson Street, one hundred blocks to the Upper West Side. The whole way, as I walked, I kept thinking one thought: *I am walking the way a survivor walks, one foot in front of the other, deliberate, on his own two feet, alone.* The farther I walked the more it seemed as if I'd walked so long that I had outlived almost everyone—even the people around me on the street seemed dead somehow, though still alive.

"It isn't just Francisco," I told Helen that night when I went to her apartment to talk. It wasn't just Francisco, though it seemed as if some memory of his body had been keeping me alive while others died. It was Larry and the way he died, also, with PCP; and Henry, with KS lesions in his lungs; and

Stanley, whose brain erupted with tumors; and Paul, with dementia—Paul, whom I had known so long I could remember when he was still straight and married.

"Married," Helen murmured. "I was married. Twice."

Not even Helen could listen, it seemed.

That night I felt as if the whole world had died, or at least the world as I had known it, though I had no black armband to wear to show what I had lost or what that world had meant to me. But that was also the night that Helen showed me the room that had been Josh's and said I could live there if I ever needed, that she'd help me if I got sick; there was no need for worry because I could stay with her if the time should come when . . .

I stood in the doorway, studying the small room, which looked stricken beneath the harsh brightness of the ceiling light—the unvarnished pine desk, the narrow bed covered with a thin blanket, the nightstand with its metal gooseneck lamp. *Well*, I thought, *it's a home, or a kind of home, at least*, and I felt happy to have it, as if I could breathe for the first time in years.

Afterward I went downtown to the Positive Immunity workshop I'd enrolled in to boost my immune system. I sat in a circle with the other men while the facilitator led us in chanting: "Living. Dying. Living. Dying. Two different words for just one thing."

I know what ritual we'll get when we die, I thought each time I looked around the room at the bunch of us, the worried unwell, the last of our kind, *Homo urbanus*. It won't be Kaddish. It won't be a funeral pyre on the Ganges. It'll be a boombox playing "Je Ne Regrette Rien" in the rear of some Unitarian church hung with rainbow flags, like a gay Knights of Columbus hall.

One of the men in our circle started coughing. At first it was just a small cough, but then it didn't stop; he just kept coughing and coughing, and we were all staring at him and thinking, *Oh, shit, TB, maybe, or pneumonia . . .*

I don't need this, I was thinking. *I don't need this. I just need to get out of here.*

I walked into the street and started home. It was a cold night, and I could see all the way up Sixth Avenue. The sidewalk was crowded with people, some walking briskly and some pausing to look at things for sale in lighted windows. *I'm an ordinary person*, I kept thinking, *I'm among the others, I'm one of them, that's who I am.* That's when it occurred to me that I'd never have to go back to that room where the man was coughing and coughing. I had a new fate now. I had Helen.

It's almost midafternoon when I spot Helen standing in the lobby, wearing her swimsuit covered with an old T-shirt that says POCONOS. She's looking through a rack of postcards.

"Where have you been?" I ask.

191

"Looking at postcards," she says.

"Since last night?"

Helen doesn't answer. We have a rule that neither of us is allowed to inquire about things about which nothing has been prevolunteered. We also have a competing rule that we're not allowed to keep secrets.

She chooses a card from the rack and examines it. "What do you think of this one?" she asks.

She says she's thinking she might send a card to Dr. Berlinski—"Thank Yahweh You're Not Here"—but I can't tell if she's kidding. Berlinski was her first oncologist, the one with whom she had an affair when she lost her hair from chemo. When he told her to take off her wig one night during sex, assuring her she'd still be beautiful, she believed God had given her Berlinski as her reward for having cancer. That was the week before Josh was killed.

"Let's go," I tell her. We're supposed to be spending the day at the dock, preparing for Josh's Yahrzeit.

"Just a minute," she says, retrieving the Panasonic cassette player from where she's left it on a sofa. She wants to bring it so we can listen to some tapes she's made of Josh's favorite music, like Lynyrd Skynyrd and Nirvana and Def Leppard doing "Pour Some Sugar on Me." Though music's forbidden on Tisha B'Av, Helen has decided these songs are special exceptions since they no longer constitute what Rabbi Stollman would call "a joyful noise." After all, they were Josh's songs, and now Josh is dead.

Down at the dock, we spread out our beach towels. Helen starts unpacking a tote bag of things she's brought along for the Yahrzeit, which we plan to observe by rowing onto the lake at dusk and lighting a candle. We can't observe it earlier than dusk, Helen tells me, since the rabbi says people should mourn and lament only after they've concluded the important daytime obligations of living, such as tending to business and making money. But we have no business to tend to, I want to tell her, other than mourning and listening to Rabbi Stollman.

"Look what I brought," she says, holding up a booklet Josh made her one Mother's Day, stapling together xeroxes of his favorite poems—*real* poems, Helen points out, like by Muriel Rukeyser and Sharon Olds and people like that, not just the junk that most kids would choose. She shows me his Yankees baseball cap and his small collection of key chains, chronicling the history of each one—how he got this key chain on a school trip to Valley Forge and this one from a Hebrew school classmate who'd visited Tel Aviv with her uncle's family. She shows me a key chain from which dangles a mini Magic 8 Ball.

As for me, I have even less than Helen, at least of Francisco's: an orange cotton handkerchief; a Zippo lighter he once bought in a junk shop, engraved with a stranger's monogram.

193

"Let me tell you what I was planning for the bar mitzvah," Helen says. She'd hired a caterer, a real first-rate outfit, sort of a kosher Balducci's: buffet dinner for sixty, with salmon steaks and fish salads, five different kinds. Helen has told me all of this before. Josh didn't live to see his bar mitzvah.

I shift on my towel. I look over the edge of the dock, down into the water. Small fish dart in and out of the shallows. For a moment, I want to tell Helen something I remembered a few nights ago—something Francisco once said, I think, though now I can't recall exactly what.

"You're not listening," she says.

"I'm listening," I tell her. But in truth I'm staring into the water, trying to remember what Francisco looked like—how his hands looked, for instance, when he touched me, and what his body looked like when he stood before the mirror, taking off his shirt. His chest was smooth and lightly muscular. I remember that.

"You want to listen to 'Pour Some Sugar on Me'?" Helen asks.

"No."

"I do," she says.

I watch her as she fiddles with the cassette player. The sun is harsh. In this light, she looks almost defeated, her arms covered with small patches of scaling skin, the residue of the psoriasis she got while undergoing chemo.

I don't want to be here, not right now, not on

this sun-struck dock, listening to Helen. For a moment, it had almost seemed as if I were in Paris again, as if I'd been traveling there simply by gazing into the reflection of my own face in Eagle Lake. I want to tell Helen how Francisco looked the last time I saw him, standing on a concrete quay in the Gare du Nord—his dark face, the radiance of his white shirt.

"I can tell you aren't listening," Helen says. She can't get the cassette player to start working, though she keeps pushing the Play button. The tape is jammed.

I don't know what to do. I don't belong here, not with these widows, not even with Helen, though I can't imagine where I do belong, not any longer.

"What?" Helen asks.

"Nothing."

"You're acting like you're mad at me," she says.

"No," I tell her.

"I think you might be pissed about the guy I met in the bar last night," she says. "I think you're jealous."

I don't want to discuss this. "It's not like we're married," I tell her.

She puts down the cassette player. "That's right," she says. "That's exactly right. It's not like we're married."

She turns away, making a display of herself, arranging Josh's things in a circle around her. *Stop it*, I want to tell her. *You're the one who gets to have a Yahrzeit. You're the one who's in remission.*

"Go ahead and be pissed if you want," she says as she works, "but don't take it out on Josh."

"I waited all morning," I answer. "I waited because of Josh." But that's not really true. I waited for Helen.

"Okay," she says. "Okay, forget it."

"It's not like I'm dead," I tell her, although as soon as I say it I realize it sounds like a non sequitur.

"No," she says. "It's not like you're dead."

Then we sit in silence, neither of us knowing what to say next. It's a draw, as it always is: Dead son trumps dead ex-lover, but AIDS trumps cancer. No matter how much the ante gets raised, no one ever wins the pot.

I stand up and start folding my towel. "I need to go," I tell her. I tell her I'm getting a headache.

"You can't," she says.

"I have to," I tell her, putting my T-shirt back on so that no one will see my unclothed torso when I get back to the lodge, now that I'm a member of the KS Club. *Helen, you'll live,* I'm thinking.

"It's Tisha B'Av," she says.

I look at her as she sits on her beach towel, holding the booklet that Josh made her, her shoulders streaked with sunburn. For a moment, I want to tell her I'm sorry. I want to tell her it isn't important, it's just a feeling I had and I'll stay, but it seems too late to say these things.

"I need to go to my room and lie down," I say. I tell her I'll meet her at dusk for the Yahrzeit.

I start up the hill.

"Don't you want to listen to *The Torah Tapes*?" Helen shouts after me. "Or don't you give a shit what happens to the Jews?"

I don't answer. I keep going, past the tennis court and through the stand of fir pines. As soon as I'm alone, it occurs to me that what I want is to drive somewhere, to drive and drive with no destination, like in the old days, though it's not until I'm climbing the front steps of the lodge that I realize that what I'd like even more is a drink. And why not? I've got my own little Yahrzeit coming up. "You've got to give up drinking," the doctor said the day I was diagnosed almost fifteen months ago, though I'd told him I drank only wine now and again. Alcohol, he said, causes the virus to replicate at twice the speed.

Well, I thought, *I knew it was good for something*.

I know I'm on dangerous ground. I know the AA commandments—they're my version of the Torah—and I know how to keep living after the world falls apart: Don't think. Don't drink. Go to meetings.

I'm just thinking of a drink because of Francisco, I tell myself—because Francisco died and then the friend who called to tell me the news died, too, a few months later, and then I no longer knew anyone who could remember Francisco and me, at least not from that time, not from back then.

I step onto the porch. The Adirondack chairs are empty, the old ladies having gone in to take their naps before preparing for dinner.

Then I see Sanjit standing in the corner.

"Hello," he says, as if he's been watching me.

"What are you doing?" I ask.

"Looking at the water," he says. He steps toward me. He points at Eagle Lake. It's late afternoon, almost evening. In this light, the water is gray and still, almost as if it were something solid.

"Sometimes I row out there," I tell him. "In a boat."

He says he likes the lake, that it reminds him of the time he once spent in the north of India, near the border of China. In that region, he says, the whole world is made of water. The earth they live upon there consists of floating islands.

He is beautiful, I'm thinking—his stillness; his calm, lean body; his serious, dark face. We're standing close to each other, our arms almost touching, though I don't know if what I'm feeling—shortness of breath, a kind of anticipatory paralysis—feels like loss or desire.

"I could take you in the boat with me," I tell him.

"I cannot put you to such a bother," he says. I can't tell if he's embarrassed by the suddenness of my invitation.

"It's no bother," I say. I don't know how to tell him he's saving me from something—from myself.

Soon we are walking the path to the boathouse. He's a few steps ahead of me, and I'm watching him as he touches a hand lightly to the honeysuckle bushes as he ambles by them. I can remember what it's like to be alive. It's simple, like pushing a button.

I ask him to choose a boat, and he picks the new one, the one painted blue, not the old one that Helen and I use. I kneel beside the boat to steady it as he steps in, seating himself in the bow. Then I untie the line and step in also, taking the middle seat, my hands on the oars. We're facing each other.

I row. I watch him. For a long time, he is silent, studying the shoreline, where late light is darkening the pines. Then he murmurs, "This is good."

When we reach the center of the lake, I lift the oars into the boat. I sit back. We drift in slow, loose circles.

I cannot stop watching him. He removes his shirt and holds it in his lap. He needs to keep it neat for dinner, he says.

I'm in no hurry to get back.

"There's an island on the lower lake we could row to," I tell him. I imagine us lying on its shore, side by side, naming the shapes we see in the clouds above us. I imagine myself telling him what has happened that has brought me here: how my friends have died and how it sometimes feels as if I alone have somehow escaped to tell the tale, though there's no one left to whom I might tell it except Helen, who has her own story to share.

He shifts in his seat. "I wish I'd brought water," he says.

I close my eyes. *This is what the revealed world has given me*, I'm thinking, *in exchange for my losses—this moment, this easeful drifting.*

When I open my eyes, I see that he is looking at me.

"What?" I ask.

"Nothing," he says.

"No, go ahead."

"I want to ask a question," he says.

I believe I know what he is thinking. It's wasn't a day-dream, my intuition about his being gay.

"It's personal," he says.

I nod. I want to encourage him.

He looks away, trailing his hand through the water. Then he looks back at me. "I am wondering about your sickness," he says.

I'm startled. "What?" I ask. "I don't know what you mean."

He can't know, or so I'm thinking. It's not as if he's seen me shirtless on the dock; it's not as if I've got what one friend used to call "the look"— drawn face and darkened eyes, the first vague traces of wasting.

"I'm wondering if you have it," he says. "You know. The virus. My mother showed me the medicine you keep in the fridge."

So there it is, in plain sight. I'd thought it was concealed within my blood, visible only if titrated. What can I say? *Please, kind sir, which virus would that be?*

"Yes," I tell him. "HIV. The virus."

He shakes his head. "I am very sorry. That is very bad." He asks if I have told my mother.

"She's dead," I tell him.

He leans forward to indicate that he wants to speak in confidence, as if there were some chance that another person might overhear. "I prefer men," he says, almost whispering. "But I have only one boyfriend because I do not wish to get this virus."

He looks at me as if he wants me to tell him something—that he'll be safe forever, perhaps.

"Please understand, my mother does not know about me," he continues. "Please understand I am telling you a secret."

But I'm not listening, not really, not any longer. I'm staring into the water. Francisco's dead, I keep telling myself. Francisco died, but not for love of me.

Then I realize: It's dusk. It's Tisha B'Av.

I tap on her door: "Helen, Helen." I can hear that she's listening to *The Torah Tapes*, though I can't make out what the rabbi is saying, only the strange but melodious singsong of his chanting.

"I want to come in," I say, but she doesn't answer.

When I open the door, I see that she's sitting cross-legged on the bed, cradling the Panasonic, rocking rapidly back and forth in what seems a kind of furious davening. The rabbi's chanting something, I'm not sure what, about seeing *chaluk*, the robes of brilliant light in which God wrapped himself so He'd be visible to Moses.

201

Helen looks up and switches off the cassette tape, severing the rabbi in mid-passage. "What?" she asks. "What do you want?"

I don't know, I want to tell her.

"I'm busy," she says, "listening to the rabbi, learning all about God's faces." She starts to talk more quickly. "I bet you didn't know He's got lots of faces, different faces, I bet you thought He had no face or that He was invisible or something like that, but no, that's not what the rabbi says . . ."

"Helen," I say.

"No," she says.

She leans back against the wall and shuts her eyes. She looks tired, her face mottled with grief. "You were supposed to be here," she says. "You were supposed to be here, but you weren't."

I sit on the bed beside her. For a moment I feel as if I'm her husband, come home late from work; I've missed something important that I've promised I'd be back in time to see—a recital, perhaps, or a school play. We're discussing our son, whom I have disappointed.

I see the Yahrzeit candle on her bureau. "You didn't light Josh's candle," I say.

"It got too late," she says.

I know the candle's supposed to be lit at sundown, as the rabbi has explained, just as soon as the day's extinguished, but I tell her that this doesn't really matter.

"It matters," she says. "It's a *ritual*."

There's nothing more to say, or so I imagine. I

can hear a car engine idling roughly outside in the parking lot. I hear an occasional door opening and shutting in the corridor.

"I've got to take my medicine," I say.

Helen nods. "Go ahead."

I stand to go, though I don't want to leave like this. "We could meet in the boathouse," I tell her.

She doesn't answer.

I go down the back stairs to the refrigerator. It now seems public, the brown paper bag that holds the vials, though I carry it up to my room, where I give myself my injection, then take two Tylenol, as I always do, to stave off side effects. When I'm done, I go downstairs, relieved to find no one sitting in the lobby.

It's dark inside the boathouse. There are only the muffled soft sounds of the rowboats striking against the rubber tires tied to the sides of the docks.

Then I see Helen, already seated in our boat, watching me.

"I didn't think you'd come," I say.

"I'm here," she says.

I step into the boat. Helen leans over to untie it, as she always does, and we push off.

There's almost no moon, though each time I row a long stroke, I can see the oars moving through the black water, as if they were pushing through darkness itself, then rising as pale emanations. I want to say a prayer. But I can't recall one.

"Look," Helen says, almost whispering. She points

to the opposite shore. Someone's walking there, among the high weeds along the embankment, shining a flashlight in the water.

"Who is it?" Helen asks.

"I don't know. Maybe someone camping in the woods."

Whoever it is walks back into the trees. For a few moments, we watch as the flashlight's beam darts through the lower branches, briefly revealing them. Then it disappears.

"I want to light the Yahrzeit candle," Helen says. She's brought it along, in her pocket. She sets it on the tip of the bow and strikes a wooden match. When she touches the match to the wick, a small flame sputters and then catches, though it makes too weak a light to guide us.

"I don't want to say Kaddish," Helen says.

"You don't have to," I tell her.

"I have to do something," she says.

"You can talk about him," I say. "You can tell me things you remember."

"No," she says, "I don't want to do that."

She says she thinks she'll sing a song; then she says she can't recall any songs to which she knows enough words. She hums "Greensleeves" instead.

I ask, "Did Josh like 'Greensleeves'?"

"I don't know," she says.

She looks out toward the shore. I can tell she's not sure what to do, that the Yahrzeit ritual isn't working.

Then she whispers, "Joshua."

She whispers it again: "Joshua, Joshua, Josh." Then she says it aloud and then louder still, until she's calling it across the lake, one letter at a time: "J-O-S-H-U-A."

But there's no Joshua. The concealed world has not returned him. There's only Helen and me sitting in a boat, a space between us.

Helen lifts the candle. It flickers but doesn't blow out. Then she holds it out over the water as if trying to look down into darkness itself. Is it true what the rabbi says, that heaven and earth were made of water? I know what Helen says about Genesis—that God didn't punish Adam by killing him but rather by letting him live.

I put down the oars. I lean over the side of the boat, but the water's too black to see through. "Who goes there, in the dark?" I whisper.

"We do," Helen answers.

ACKNOWLEDGMENTS

For their sustaining support, I thank the National Endowment for the Arts, the D.C. Commission on the Arts, American University, the Jenny McKean Moore Fund for Writers, the Fine Arts Work Center in Provincetown, the Corporation of Yaddo, The MacDowell Colony, the Virginia Center for the Creative Arts, the Djerassi Foundation, and the Blue Mountain Center.

I also thank Jerome Badanes (d. 1995), Ellen Geist, Wesley Gibson, Andrew Holleran, Joanne Jacobson, Anne Dabney Richardson, and Ralph Sassone, for their valuable comments on various drafts of these stories; Richard Bausch, for his early encouragement; Tillie Olsen, for her heartening support and inspiring example; David Burton, for serving as my loving and reliable "guardian of solitude" (to borrow a phrase from Rilke) while I was finishing this book; Marianne Merola and Joanne Brownstein, of Brandt and Hochman, for their generosity and hard work; Rahel Lerner, Suzanne Williams, and all the wonderful people at Pantheon Books, for their enthusiasm and dedication; and, above all, Gail

Hochman and Dan Frank, for their loyalty, intelligence, patience, and belief.

Finally, I want to thank the many extraordinary people, including numerous physicians, surgeons, and health care workers, who saw me through a long illness and the liver transplant surgery that allowed me to complete this book so long in the making. In particular, I want to thank my dear brother, Jeff, and the beloved friends and found family who cared for me during that time, including Sarah Priestman, Joanne Jacobson, Gregory Arms, Susan Elg, Nick Flynn, Wesley Gibson, Amy Gussack, Charlotte Hays, Tony Hoagland, Carole Horn, Marie Howe, Thérèse Jones, Karen Kevorkian, Matt Klam, Susan Marcisz, Bert Menninga, Faye Moskowitz, Kermit Moyer, Bill O'Sullivan, Sky Power, Maxine Rodburg, Tim Rogers, Jane Stanley, Jean Valentine, Bobbi Whalen, and Linda Woolford. From them I learned, as Brenda Hillman writes in her poem "Quartz Tractate," "It is the job of the living to be seen through."

The author is grateful to the editors of the following magazines and anthologies in which these stories first appeared, sometimes in slightly different form:

"Crêpe de Chine" first appeared in *Ms. Magazine*.

"My Mother's Clothes: The School of Beauty and Shame" first appeared in *The Atlantic*. Reprinted in *Editor's Choice: Best New Fiction for 1987* (Bantam, 1987), *Men on Men 2: Best New Gay Fiction* (New American Library, 1988), *How We Live Now: Contemporary Multicultural Literature* (Bedford, 1992), *The Penguin Book of Gay Short Stories* (Penguin, 1994), *First Sightings: Stories of American Youth* (Persea, 1994), *Lavender Mansions: Forty Gay and Lesbian Stories* (Westview Press, 1994), *Mama's Boy: Gay Men Write About Their Mothers* (Painted Leaf Press, 2000), *I Know Some Things: Contemporary Writers on Childhood* (Faber & Faber, 2000), and *Worlds of Fiction* (Macmillan, 2001).

"Dream House" first appeared in *Ploughshares* as "Shelters."

Portions of "Snapshots of the Visible Man" first

appeared in *New Virginia Review* as "Covenants: Scenes for a Novel" and in *Ghost Letters* (Alice James Books, 1994) as "The Night He Died."

"Some Threads Through the Medina" first appeared in *Men on Men 5: Best New Gay Fiction* (Dutton, 1994).

"Fugitive Light, Old Photos" first appeared in *American Short Fiction*. Reprinted in *Listening to Ourselves: More Stories from National Public Radio's "The Sound of Writing"* (Doubleday, 1994) and in *Survival Stories: Memoirs of Crisis* (Doubleday, 1998).

"Eduardo's Hair" first appeared under a different title in *Too Darn Hot:Writing About Sex Since Kinsey* (Persea, 1998).

"The Universe, Concealed" first appeared in *Poz Magazine*. Reprinted in *Men on Men 2000: Best New Gay Fiction* (Plume, 2000).

Grateful acknowledgment is made to the following for permission to reprint previously published material:

HarperCollins Publishers Inc.: Excerpt from the poem "Childhood" from *Selected Poems of Rainer Maria Rilke*, edited and translated by Robert Bly. Copyright © 1981 by Robert Bly. Reprinted by permission of HarperCollins Publishers Inc.

Warner Bros. Publications U.S. Inc.: Excerpt from the song lyric "Star Dust" by Hoagy Carmichael and Mitchell Parish. Copyright © 1929 (Renewed 1957) by EMI Mills Music, Inc. and Hoagy